Gertie's Real Life Adventures

Gertie's Real Life Adventures

JANE DAHL

EDITED BY
LOIS FEINBERG-GONZENBACH

RESOURCE *Publications* · Eugene, Oregon

Resource Publications
A Division of Wipf and Stock Publishers
199 W. 8th Ave., Suite 3
Eugene, OR 97401
www.wipfandstock.com

ISBN 13: 978-1-49825-198-3

Manufactured in the U.S.A.

Names, characters, places, and incidents are based on actual people and events which occurred at the turn of the twentieth century.

All Scripture references are from the King James Bible. Some references have been paraphrased.

In loving memory of
Mabel Gertrude Foster

whose sharing of her real life experiences
made it possible
for Gertie to share hers

Contents

List of Illustrations

Preface

THE LIFE AND TIMES of Gertie Larson reflect many differences from the life and times of today's children. Yet one similarity stands out: the children of today are blessed with the same freedom to live by faith in God, and in His Son, Jesus, as children in Gertie's day.

May Gertie's story illustrate this wonderful similarity that neither time nor circumstance has altered, and may this similarity, with God's continued blessing, remain in the lives of our children forever.

Acknowledgments

From the time that *Gertie's Real Life Adventures* first began to sprout from seeds planted in my mother's childhood memories, I've been encouraged by members of my family, especially my husband, Don. As the years passed, friends came alongside to join in prayer, reading and re-reading my manuscript, and in offering helpful suggestions. This constant encouragement pruned and cultivated the tender sprouting seeds as they grew and blossomed into *Gertie's* story.

If I were to mention all of my encouragers by name, not only would the list be pages long, but there would be the unthinkable possibility of forgetting to name some deserving family member or friend. So, I simply offer my heartfelt thanks to them all.

There are a few, however, whose special talents, experience, and help make their individual acknowledgments a must: Pastor Larry Adams, for affirming ten-year-old Gertie's simple understanding of the Bible and its teachings; Phillip Bird, for his expert computer assistance; "Skip" Brey, for her creative and story enhancing ideas; Ken and Carole Lowy, for their valuable help and suggestions; and Pastor Rick Moe, for his assurance that the Gospel message, as presented through Gertie and her real life adventures, is right on!

To all I say, "God bless you, every one!"

And to my heavenly Father, the greatest encourager and helper of all, thank You for those countless times You broke through my writer's block to give me deeper insight, or new ideas, or just a better word to use, or a better way to turn a phrase. May You use this story of a little ten-year-old girl and her family to bless other children and their families in whatever ways You choose. Amen!

ADVENTURE 1

1

A Little About Me

HELLO. MY NAME IS Gertrude Anne Larson. Everybody calls me Gertie. I was born here in Richfield, Utah, on September 23, 1894. I'll save you the trouble of figuring it out, I'm ten years old. Actually, almost eleven.

I live with my family in rooms above our place of business, The Richfield Restaurant. There's lots of chores to running a restaurant. Like Mama cooks for the customers all day long. Good news is, she doesn't have to cook for us. We eat whatever's left on the stove after the customers get their fill. Bad news is, sometimes there's not much left on the stove.

Me and my sisters, Mary and Pauline, set the tables with a knife, fork, and spoon, and fill the salt and pepper shakers. Papa stands at the door and greets the customers.

"Welcome, folks!" he says, and points them to a table. Then he takes their orders. Then he brings their food. Then he takes their money.

Our biggest job is scraping and scrubbing the stacks and stacks of dirty dishes. We could dearly use another pair of hands in the dishpan, but our baby sister, Lorraine, is too little to help. She's good for business though. We put her in her buggy, tie a ribbon in her hair, make sure her nose isn't runny and her diaper's dry, and roll her into the dining room. She sits there smiling and cooing at the customers. They love her.

When I was seven years old, something bigger than all our chores put together happened to me. The Preacher of the Baptist Church said I was a sinner. At seven I was too little to know all that "sinner" meant, but from the way the Preacher said it, I knew it wasn't good. He said if I asked Jesus, He'd forgive my sins and be my Savior. At seven I was too little to know all that "Savior" meant, but from the way the Preacher said it, I knew it was good and something I needed. So, on Sunday, August 12, 1902, on my knees, looking up to heaven, feeling kind of shy, but happy as a lark, I asked Jesus to forgive me for any bad things I'd done, and come into my heart and be my

Savior. I wanted to be baptized right then so folks would know I belonged to Jesus, but the big tub that folks get dunked in sprung a leak. That didn't stop the Preacher! The following Sunday, with the leak still leaking, he marched the congregation down to the horse trough in back of The Workingman's Store. He said it didn't matter where you were baptized just so long as you were. At first I wasn't happy to be dipped in water horses slobber in. But after they dumped the old water out, scrubbed the boards with a stiff brush and soap, and filled the trough with fresh water, it seemed as good a place as any to be baptized. I'll never forget my baptism. I'll never forget that trough.

Now, what about you? Did you ever have the chicken pox? I did. I itched awful bad. Mama tied stockings over my hands to keep me from scratching and getting pock marks. Can you whistle? I can. Papa says I can whistle better than any boy in town. To be honest, I think it's because of that hole between my two upper front teeth. Do you know what you want to be when you grow up? I do. When I grow up, I'm gonna join the circus and be a trapeze star!

I hope in sharing a little about me, you'll see why I did, or didn't do, some of the things I did, or didn't do, in the story I'm gonna tell. It's a story 'bout three real life adventures I ended up smack dab in the middle of.

I hope you like my story. I hope you like real life adventures.

2

Real Life Adventures

HAVE YOU EVER HAD a real life adventure? Something you never dreamed could happen? Something so special you knew you'd never forget it? Some adventures spring up overnight like asparagus poppin' up in a vegetable garden; some grow slow over weeks and months like acorns takin' root in a forest. It's one of these slow-growing adventures I'm gonna tell you about first.

It starts on a sunny Saturday morning two weeks before my tenth birthday. I'm standing on my tippytoes in Mrs. Goosley's apple orchard. It's one of the places I go to practice my trapeze tricks. You know, for when I join the circus.

I reach up, grab a sturdy limb, and swing my legs up through my arms 'til I'm hanging upside-down by my knees. The blood rushing to my head helps me to think. This morning I need lots of blood pounding in my brain to help me think of a birthday activity for my birthday party. With my birthday just 'round the corner, thinking of a birthday activity is even more important than practicing my trapeze tricks.

Birthday activities are something my best friend, Ella Neil, thought up. They're not party games like Pin-The-Tale-On-The-Donkey or Button, Button, Who's Got The Button. They're more, much more than that. Birthday activities are extra fun and exciting things the party giver thinks up for her guests to do to make her party extra fun and exciting. Ella says, "The most important event in life is being born. Only trouble is, folks don't remember being born. Ask any man, woman or child what being born was like. Every last one of them will tell you, 'I don't know. I don't remember.' So we have birthday parties to help us remember we were born. The most important part of the party is the birthday activity. It's more important than the birthday cake, or the ice cream, or even the presents." Leastwise, that's what Ella says.

Ella's birthday activities have made her the most popular party giver in all of Richfield. For days 'n days after her parties, her guests are still oohing and ahhing over her birthday activities. Sad to say, my birthday comes exactly one week after hers. Every year I have to listen to my guests go on and on about Ella's birthday activity the week before. Like for her birthday activity last year, she led her guests on a nature hunt in the meadow east of the railroad station.

"Whoever finds the most interesting rock or flower or other natural wonder wins this prize," she told us, and waved a thin, square box wrapped in pink paper under our noses. Then she shouted, "Go!" and off we all scampered to hunt for prize winning natural wonders.

I'd just slipped some pretty white pebbles I found into the pocket of my dress when Alice Brown came thrashing through the meadow grass. Her eyes were bugged out and her tongue flapping. *"Run for your lives!"* she screamed. *"It's Wilson's bull! He's loose and he's headed this way!"*

Just a hop, skip and a jump behind Alice came Wilson's bull, thrashing through the meadow grass. His eyes were bugged out and his tongue flapping. 'Round and around we stumbled, pushing and bumping into each other to get out of his way.

That's when Ella pointed at the railroad station and yelled, "Follow me!" Then off she galloped, whooping and waving her bonnet in the air. Then off we galloped after her, screaming and crying. Then off the bull galloped after us, snorting and bellowing!

I'll never forget standing on the station platform, watching Mr. Wilson and his two boys trying to rope the wild-eyed, slobbering animal. Every time the ropes slipped off the bull's sweaty body and onto the ground, Ella led us in clapping and cheering. *For the bull!* Now that we were safe on the station platform, tears and fears changed to cheers. Except for me. 'Cause by then I'd figured it out. *Ella arranged for that bull to get loose!* How else could she act so brave when the bull came stampeding into her nature hunt? Yes, sir, I bet that bull didn't just happen to join Ella's birthday activity. Nobody's that lucky. Not even Ella. (The prize that day for the most interesting rock or flower or other natural wonder was a box of pink embroidered handkerchiefs, won by Alice Brown.)

The following week was my birthday party. All that my guests could talk about was Ella's party. While they went on and on about her "exciting" birthday activity, they dipped dinner knives into a bowl of vanilla frosting and spread it on the gingerbread men Mama baked the night before. That was my birthday activity—frosting gingerbread men. Bet you can guess whose birthday party was a real life adventure. Bet you can guess whose wasn't. Bet you can guess why I'm trying hard now, as I hang upside-down in Mrs. Goosley's orchard, to think of a birthday activity that'll make my party as fun and exciting as Ella's party's bound to be.

All at once, an idea starts to pound inside my brain. Why not have my birthday activity right here in Mrs.Goosley's orchard? We can take turns to see who can hang upside-down the longest! No one's ever had a tree hanging birthday activity before. All I have to do is ask Mrs.Goosley.

I look down the rows of apple trees. There in the middle of the orchard sits Mrs. Goosley's yellow frame house. Upside-down, it looks like the giant head of a clown: the roof's a brown grinning mouth; the chimney a red snaggletooth; the windows, with their partly drawn shades, two half-opened eyes; and the front door a shiny green nose. Just then, the nose flies open and out blows Mrs. Goosley onto her porch. Her high top shoes scoot across the wooden boards above her while her head bounces along below like a lively rubber ball. Leastwise, that's what she looks like topsy-turvy. She cups her hands around her mouth and yells at me, "Ger . . . son . . . ge . . . dow . . . te . . . yo . . . fa!"

By now the blood's pounding so loud in my ears, I can't tell what she's saying. Better get right-side-up and see what she wants, I figure. I slip myself down between my arms 'til I'm hanging head up, feet dangling.

"Ma'am?" I call politely.

"I said," shouts Mrs. Goosley, "if you don't get down from that tree, Gertie Larson, I'm going to tell your father on you! I'm tired of you children climbing in my orchard, breaking off my branches, and stealing my apples!" She whirls 'round, her long skirt flying, and stomps back inside the house. The "nose" bangs shut behind her.

With all her shouting, stomping, and banging, I know she'll never let me have my birthday activity in her precious old orchard now. I'm back right where I started. No fun and exciting birthday activity that'll make my party as fun and exciting as Ella's party's bound to be. Problems, problems.

3

More Problems

As I skip up Main Street on my way to the restaurant, Mrs. Goosley's yelling is still hollerin' in my ears. I wish I'd told her I never stole any of her precious old apples. True, I've taken one now and then. But I never meant it as stealing. Course, if it *looks* like stealing, I'd better leave her old apples alone. I don't want to do anything that looks bad to others. Not even to Mrs. Goosley.

"Yoo-hoo, Gertie!" It's Ella calling from the corner up ahead. She's waving and jumping up and down. Looks like she's worked up about something.

The minute I'm standing beside her, she grabs my arm, "Oh, Gertie, I have the most wonderful news! The circus is coming! It gets here the day before your birthday!"

(Have you ever had somebody come up to you, hand you a silver dollar, tip his hat, and go on his way? Me neither. But when Ella tells me the news about the circus, I feel just the way I'd feel if somebody dropped a silver dollar in my hand.)

"The circus! Are you sure?" I ask, afraid it's too good to be true.

Ella's head bobs up and down. "They're starting to put up circus posters all over town."

I wet my lips, pucker them in a circle, curl my tongue, suck in a breath, and blow out a whistle Papa would be proud of. Then I say, "With the circus coming the day before my birthday, this will be the most wonderful birthday anybody has ever had!"

The minute I say it, I'm sorry. Ella believes with all her heart that her birthdays are the most wonderful of anybody's. If anybody says different, she takes it real serious.

Sure enough, her peachy cheeks turn red. "Well . . . well . . . well," she says, like she's trying to work a knot out of her tongue. "I just hope the circus won't *spoil* your birthday." Her eyes are squinty.

"*Spoil* my birthday? How can the circus *spoil* my birthday?" I ask her.

"Well, with the circus coming the day before your birthday, everybody will have their minds on the circus. *Not* on your party. Unless, of course," and her eyes get squintier, "you plan a birthday activity as exciting as a circus act."

I feel like I'm gonna be sick.

"I gotta get to the restaurant," I tell her. I know if I don't get away from her quick, I'll prob'ly say something she'll have to forgive me for later.

As I hurry up the street, I look back. Ella's twirlin' around on her toes like those fancy dancers in short frothy skirts. I can't see her face for all her twirlin'. But I know Ella. She's likely grinning from ear to ear.

When I get to the restaurant, Mama's busy at the stove stirring a big pot of chicken soup for the customers' dinner. She picks up a bowl of dough, scoops out a spoonful and drops it into the bubbling broth. The lump sinks to the bottom, then floats to the top, fluffing into a tasty Danish dumpling.

Mama sees me staring at the pot. "Gertie, take the bucket and get some water from the spillway. You can have a dumpling when you get back."

The promise of a dumpling gets me moving. I grab the bucket from the peg beside the back door and hurry through the empty dining room to the front door. Out on Main Street I turn right toward Third Street. There on the corner of Main and Third, water from a ditch that runs along Third Street is pumped up through a pipe into a wooden trough. The trough is called "the spillway." Business folks along Main Street use water from the spillway if they don't have a well of their own. We don't have a well of our own.

As I skip along, I see Sammy Stevens up ahead. He's standing in the middle of the small wooden footbridge that leads over the ditch to the spillway. Though I'm not afraid of many things, Sammy Stevens is one of them. He's big as an ox and mean as Wilson's bull. Mama says he can't help the way he is, that something happened to his brain when he was born. She says we should be nice to him. I say that's easier said than to do. 'Specially now with him blocking my way. His legs are spread out like tree trunks dressed in overalls. His copper colored hair is shimmering in the sun like tiny flames of fire. He's as scary a sight as you'd ever want to see. If it wasn't for that dumpling Mama promised me, I'd leave filling my bucket for a time when Sammy's not around. But I know an empty bucket won't get me that dumpling. So, I suck in a big breath and keep heading for the spillway. Maybe if I don't bother him, he won't bother me. But, sad to say, the minute I climb onto the footbridge, Sammy comes at me, jabbing his fists in the air. "I'm gonna throw you in the ditch!" he yells at me.

Though I'm not afraid of many things, drowning is one of them. The water in the ditch is deep enough to drown in if you don't know how to swim. I don't know how to swim.

I look up and down the street for somebody to help me. There's only a couple of old ladies staring at the hats in the millinery shop window. A lot of good they could do me. That's when I think of something Papa and Mama said 'bout what a struggle it must be to raise a child like Sammy. Papa said, "Since Mrs. Stevens died ten years ago, and Sammy only three at the time, Mr. Stevens has tried to be a good father. He wants Sammy to behave so folks will like him."

"Yes," Mama said, "but he disciplines him pretty hard. He's even sent him to bed without any supper."

Thinking of what Papa and Mama said gives me an idea. I stamp my foot down hard so Sammy'll know I mean business. "If you throw me in that ditch and I drown, I'll tell your father on you."

Sammy's big body slumps all over. "Don't tell my father, please," he begs, "I'll be good."

I plainly have the upper hand. I know what I should do—fill my bucket and head back to the restaurant. But what the Preacher said the day I was baptized turns out to be true. "Even if you receive Jesus as your Savior and are baptized, your old sinful nature can still get the best of you if you don't fight it tooth and nail."

What the Preacher meant was that you have to fight your old sinful nature with your whole body, from your teeth to your toenails. Leastwise, that's what I think he meant. Course with the fancy way preachers talk, you can't always be sure.

Well, I plainly let my old sinful nature get the best of me this day. Instead of tending to my bucket business and going on my way, I say to Sammy, "I won't tell your father on you if you get down on your knees and pray."

Now, there's nothing wrong with praying. God wants us to pray. But I know what prayer Sammy'll pray. It's a prayer the bratty boys taught him. Those bratty boys. There's a dozen or so of them, and they're all ornery. That's why I call them "bratty." They taught Sammy the prayer to tease and torment him. It's a silly prayer, a prayer you'd never pray to God. But Sammy doesn't know it, because of his hurt brain. He thinks he's talking to God. All he's doing is giving the bratty boys somebody to torment and laugh at.

I point to the boards on the footbridge. Sammy falls down on his knees. He folds his hands under his chin, shuts his eyes, bows his head, and prays, "Father bake a cake, father bake a cake, father bake a cake. Amen."

While he says his silly prayer over and over, I slip around him, fill my bucket in the spillway, slip back around him, step down off the footbridge, and head up the street to the restaurant. As I hurry along, a voice inside me keeps whispering, "Gertie, shame on you. Gertie, shame on you. Gertie, shame on you." I know it's my conscience scolding me. Papa says God gives us a conscience so we'll know if something's right to do or something's wrong to do; that a conscience is there to help keep us out of trouble. Even so, there are times I'd just as soon not have one. Like now.

When I get to the restaurant, Mama's busy at the stove with her back to me. I slide the bucket onto the table and tippytoe up the stairs to my bedroom. I don't want her to see me. She has a way of knowing when I do something wrong. I don't know how she knows. She just knows. I figure it's a special gift God gives to mamas. I crawl out my window onto the balcony that faces on Main Street. I look down toward the spillway. There's Sammy still kneeling on the footbridge. Only now he's not alone. Three bratty boys are standing over him, laughing and slapping each other on the back. Sammy's rocking to and fro on his knees. It looks like he's crying. Poor Sammy. I know it's my fault he's on his knees. I know it's because he's on his knees that the bratty boys are teasing and tormenting him. I feel awful.

Later, I'm barely able to eat the dumpling Mama saved for me.

4

The Bratty Boys

BEFORE I GO ON with my story, I want to tell you a little more about the bratty boys. They're always stirring up things. Sad to say, that's why you hear more about them than you do about Richfield's good boys. Which figures when you think about it.

Papa says every town has its bratty boys. He says he was a bratty boy once himself. But after Grandpa Larson hauled him off to the woodshed a few times, and laid a switch to his backside, he pretty much got over his orneriness. Guess Grandpa Larson took to heart what the Bible says, "He that spareth his rod hateth his son." Even so, I can't see my papa being a bratty boy. He's the most loving, gentle papa in the whole wide world. Guess those trips to the woodshed did him some good.

Richfield's bratty boys must never have been hauled off to the woodshed. Leastwise, not often enough. They're always causing trouble. Like splattering you with bits of chewed up paper, pushing the smaller children around, making Sammy cry, and teasing us girls. My school teacher, Miss Goldbranson, says when a boy teases you it means he likes you. She's awful smart. But I'm not sure she's smart about this. Like the bratty boys call me "Gingersnaps" because of my freckles. They know it makes me mad. If they really liked me, would they want to make me mad? That's dumb. No, I think bratty boys are just plain bullies. It makes them feel big to make somebody else feel bad. Yes, sir, that's a bully for you. The only friends they have are each other. If you ask me, that's nothing to brag about.

You're prob'ly wondering, "What's all this got to do with Gertie's real life adventure? When do we get to the adventure part?" It's coming, believe me. You don't just jump into the middle of one. A real life adventure builds and grows out of the little things that happen every day. When we finally come to the adventure part, you'll see how all of the things I'm telling you about now are the stepping stones to get us there. Like what happened the day after I had that trouble with Sammy at the spillway.

Dinner's over, the customers' and ours. It's almost three o'clock by the time we wash and dry the last dirty dish. I'm about to leave for Ella's for some business we have to tend to at the railroad station. But before I can get out the door, Papa calls the family together. We sit down 'round the big kitchen table. The oil cloth cover is still damp where Mary wiped it off after we got through eating. It feels nice and cool on my bare arms.

"With the circus here in two weeks," Papa starts, "we'll all have to pitch in and work twice as hard." Me, Mary, and Pauline make unhappy noises. Mama shushes us with a finger to her lips. Papa gives her a "thank you" smile and goes on, "Folks will be coming from all over the county. You can bet they'll want a hot meal instead of a cold circus hot dog. We'll need to keep the hot water reservoir on the back of the stove filled, check the salt and pepper shakers often, clear off the tables the minute customers get through eating, and most of all, keep ahead of the dirty dishes." He sucks in a big breath. "Well, that about covers it. Just remember, though we'll be extra busy, if we all pitch in, we'll get along fine."

As soon as Papa stops talking, I head out the door for Ella's. Like my family, she and her folks live in rooms at their place of business—The Richfield Funeral Parlor. I figure her family won't need a meeting like my family just had. The circus won't cause them any extra work. Leastwise, I can't see how it would. Or could. Or should.

When I get to Ella's, I tippytoe through the big double doors. Empty caskets are lined up along the back wall. One has the lid open showing white silky padding inside. I feel sad and happy at the same time. Sad because those caskets won't stay empty. Happy because those very caskets are why me and Ella are best friends.

It happened like this: when Ella's family moved to Richfield three years ago, there'd never been a funeral parlor in town before. If somebody died, he was just kept at home 'til his funeral and burial. When Ella's folks opened the funeral parlor, the idea of somebody making a living out of dying caused a lot of giggling 'round the school yard.

One day at recess a couple of bratty boys were teasing Ella about her family's business. "A dead body here, a dead body there, here a body, there a body..." Ella's face got red and her eyes got watery. I didn't know her very well yet, but I couldn't let those bratty boys treat her mean. So I yelled at them, "You leave her alone!" Then I took her by the hand and walked her back to class.

From that day on, Ella treated me like her best friend. It didn't take long 'til I felt the same about her. Ella doesn't mind that my folks don't have much, or that I wear Mary's hand-me-downs, or that I wait on customers and wash dirty dishes. Oh, we've had our troubles getting along. Ella's an only child, and more than a little spoiled. She always wants to be first and best in everything. Especially birthday activities. Remember Wilson's bull? Even so, I know I can always count on her to be my friend.

When I get to the door of the living quarters, Ella's waiting for me. "Did you bring a penny, and did you shine it up good?" she asks me.

I nod, and hold my penny up for her to see

We tippytoe back through the funeral parlor. It's those caskets. They make you want to tippytoe. But once out on Main Street, we start skipping and skip all the way to the railroad station. The minute we get there, we lay our pennies side by side on the railroad tracks. And just in time. Off in the distance the train whistle's calling to let folks know the Denver and Rio Grande is rollin' into Richfield!

While the train is stopped, we pick up our pennies. The engine's heavy metal wheels have flattened them into shiny golden ovals. We stick our treasures in the pockets of our dresses, then cross the tracks into the meadow beyond.

As we stroll along, Ella goes on and on about Mr. Browning's funeral. "It's going to be lovely," she says, "He's being buried in his band uniform."

It does sound nice. But I can't get too excited about a funeral. Not with the circus coming. The circus comes only once every two or three years. We can have a funeral any time. Now, I don't mean a funeral's not important. When somebody dies, a funeral's very important. Grandma Larson says, "A funeral's our way of saying goodbye to a loved one. If that loved one has Jesus in his heart, it can even be a happy goodbye 'cause then we know that someday we'll see that loved one again in heaven." (Just the same, if I had to pick between a circus and a funeral, I wouldn't pick the funeral.)

Up ahead Aunt Danny's cow, Bossy, is standing knee-deep in meadow grass. Her big bottom jaw is going 'round and around as she munches her dinner. Out flops her tongue and slurps up some leftovers hanging from her chin. We laugh and wade through the grass to pet her.

Ella scratches Bossy's ear. "Wonder how it'd be to ride a cow."

I rub Bossy's bony behind. "Bet it would be fun."

Right then and there we make up our minds to try it. With lots of pushin', pullin', and gruntin' we scramble onto Bossy's back. Then I give her a hardy poke with my heels. And off we go!

Sad to say, riding a cow isn't as much fun as I figured it'd be. With every bouncing step, Bossy's sharp hip bones cut into my not-too-padded self. But it's an awful pretty day. Tiny puffs of clouds, like bits of down from angels' wings, sail across the sea-blue sky. Tucked here and there in the tall golden meadow grass, wild pink roses, yellow sunflowers, and lavender lady's-slippers nod their heads as we pass. Even the bees buzzing 'round us seem to be humming a happy tune.

All at once, Bossy lets out a big "MA-OOOOOOO!" like she's in some kind of pain. Maybe the bees aren't so happy after all, I'm thinking.

Then off Bossy gallops like a runaway black and white spotted locomotive, stomping the wild pink roses, knocking over the yellow sunflowers, and squashing the lavender lady's-slippers. Up ahead I see an irrigation ditch. Bossy will have to stop now. But Bossy doesn't even slow down. Her hoofs hit the slippery side of the ditch, and she sails into the air like a spotted balloon. Down she comes, landing with a splash in the muddy irrigation water. Then grunting and snorting, she digs her way up the other side. Only now she's missing a passenger. Me.

By the time I crawl, slipping and sliding, out of the ditch, Bossy is highballing across the meadow headed for home. Ella is screaming and clinging to her neck. Poor Ella. She'll have some story to tell when she gets back to the barn, I figure. And knowing Ella, she'll tell it over and over and over again. I feel sorry for Aunt Danny. She'll be the first one to hear it, over and over and over again.

That afternoon I do a lot of thinking. I think about being dumped in the irrigation ditch, which lucky for me was only half full of water. And how just the day before, I outsmarted Sammy from throwing me into just such a ditch. The more I think about the unkind way I treated him, the more I want to make things right with him. I don't know how I'll do it, but as I head for the restaurant I mean to find a way.

5

Ella's Party

ALL THAT THINKING I did in the meadow that afternoon got me to remembering, too. Like I remembered how I once added up the ages of Mama and Papa, Grandma and Grandpa Larson, and Aunt Danny. The sum came to over 200 years! That's a lot of living. You can learn a lot about life from your family. Actually, your home is like a school. But instead of reading, writing, and arithmetic, you study sharing, forgiveness, love, chores (lots about chores), patience, faith, and obedience. Family things like that. Course most families have a thing or two you're better off not to learn. Like Grandpa Larson's temper. He's a dear man, but he does get upset now and then. He's working on his temper, though. So is Grandma Larson. That's what I was remembering in the meadow that afternoon. After I got through thinking.

The week before Ella's birthday drags by with not much goin' on except for an uncommon amount of dirty dishes. Then Saturday comes at last. I wake up with the happy thought that it's Ella's birthday today, and mine's just a week away!

Since Mrs. Goosley chased me out of her apple orchard, along with my tree hanging idea, I haven't come up with another birthday activity. But I'm still working on it. Maybe Ella's party will give me an idea.

I can hear Mama singing to Lorraine down the hall. *"There's a wee little man in a wee little house, lives over the way you see. And he sits by his window and he sews all day, making shoes for you and me..."*

I think of how I'll be the one singing to Lorraine while the circus is here. Mama'll be too busy cooking for the crowds coming for miles around to see the trapeze acts, clowns, and wild animals. The song Mama's singing, "Wee Little Man," is my most favorite one. I listen for the part where she pounds her fist into the palm of her hand like a hammer. It always makes the baby laugh.

"*With a rap-a-tap-tap, and a rap-a-tap-tap, goes his hammer one, two, three. With a rap-a-tap-tap, and a rap-a-tap-tap, making shoes for you and me.*"

Lorraine squeals. She likes to rap-a-tap-tap, too, with her fat baby hands. She's barely a year old, but she's awful smart.

When the song's over, I get dressed and crawl out my window onto the balcony. The sun is shining. The sky is bright blue. It's an awful pretty day for Ella's party. Up and down Main Street the butcher shop, hardware store, saloon, ice cream parlor, and other businesses are opening for the day. Here comes Miss Goldbranson hurrying up the sidewalk. Looks like she's headed for the hotel. Bet she's meeting her sweetheart, Mr. Tannehill, for breakfast. I've heard the hotel dining room has potted palms, linen tablecloths, and a cook who can't speak English. Miss Goldbranson prob'ly likes to eat there 'cause it's fancier than our small plain restaurant. But I bet our food is better.

Just then I see Sammy stooping to peek under the swinging doors of the saloon. Someone inside yells, "Get away from here, crazy!" Poor Sammy. He shuffles up the street and stops again, this time in front of the ice cream parlor. His shoulders heave up and down. I figure he's sniffing the sweet smells of chocolate, vanilla, and marshmallow. I like to peek in the saloon, and sniff the sweet smells of the ice cream parlor, too. Guess we're not so different after all, me and Sammy.

I take a last look up and down the street. A few days ago, Mr. Browning's funeral marched up the street on its way to the cemetery. In a few days, the circus parade will march down the street to let folks know the circus is set-up at the ballpark and ready to go! It's like my Sunday School teacher, Mr. Tannehill, says, "Life has its sad times and life has its happy times. It's just the way life is." Even so, a funeral and a circus parade marching up and down the same street give me goose bumps just to think 'bout it.

I crawl back inside my room. I pull my cigar box from under my bed. All of my treasures are inside: six hand-painted china buttons on a card Grandma Larson gave me, the rattles off the rattlesnake Ella's grandpa caught, killed, and cooked for her birthday activity at Eagle Tree two years ago—he gave me the rattles 'cause I was the only guest who didn't get sick to my stomach—and last, my birthday present for Ella. A bottle of perfume. I feel proud of my present even though I didn't actually buy it. A traveling salesman who eats at our restaurant gave sample bottles to me, Mama, and Mary the last time he came traveling through Richfield.

I take the piece of shelf paper Mama said I could have, lay it on the floor, and set the bottle in the middle. Then I fold the paper over it from top to bottom, side to side, and tie it with a bit of yellow yarn. It looks real nice.

Later that afternoon when I get to Ella's, I tippytoe through the funeral parlor to the living quarters at the rear. Two other guests are there ahead of me. We knock on the door together.

"Welcome, ladies," Mr. Neil says, opening the door. He bends double at his waist and sweeps his arm toward the living room for us to come in. Mama calls Mr. Neil "elegant." I figure in his business he has to be.

He takes our presents into the kitchen. Through the doorway I can see an ice cream freezer, six mason jars filled with flowers, and a birthday cake all standing on the kitchen table. He sets our presents next to the cake.

When the last two guests arrive, Ella says, "We're going to play Musical Chairs."

Mr. Neil drags five chairs to the middle of the room, one less than us five guests and Ella. He faces three chairs one way, two the other. Mrs. Neil takes hold of the handle on the Busy Bee phonograph, gives it a couple of cranks, and slips a music cylinder into place.

"Now, make a circle around the chairs," Ella orders.

And we do.

When the music starts, we march 'round and around the chairs to the happy tune of "Yankee Doodle." All at once the music stops. We leap for a chair. Everybody lands where they're aiming 'cept Margaret Anne Ainsworth who lands on the floor. Tripped there by Ella.

After Margaret Anne and one chair are dragged away, the music starts again. 'Round and around we march. This time when the music stops it's Penny Peterson who gets bumped out of the way. With an elbow to her back. Again by Ella. Now there are four players and three chairs. Mrs. Neil rewinds the phonograph. The game goes on.

Ella's next two pushes put the Teeter twins, first Tilly, then Lilly, on the sofa with Margaret Anne Ainsworth and Penny Peterson. That leaves me, Ella, and one chair standing in the middle of the room.

After seeing the other guests tripped, bumped, and pushed out of the game, I have no hope of beating Ella. Not the way she plays Musical Chairs. But just as the music starts, she whispers, "I'm gonna let you win." Sure enough, when the music stops I feel a shove. But instead of landing on the floor like the others, I land on the chair! Sometimes Ella's a real pain. But most of the time she's a real friend.

"Here's your prize, Gertie," she says, and hands me a Feed-The-World Chocolate Bar. I slip the candy into my pocket. I don't want to eat it in front of the other guests. That wouldn't be polite. Besides, they don't look too happy.

Ella skips to the middle of the room and whirls 'round and around like an actress on a stage. "Now for my birthday activity."

This is what I've been waiting for! I'm so excited, the muscles in my back bunch up. I'm afraid I'll have to go home so Mama can knead them loose with her fist. But I make my shoulders sag. Happily, my back muscles do the same. And just in time.

"We're going to the cemetery," Ella says, "to decorate the graves of the less fortunate in Potter's Field." She looks up at the ceiling like she's looking straight through it into heaven.

So that's what the mason jars of flowers are for, I say to myself. Leave it to Ella. She really knows her birthday activities.

Mrs. Neil hands each of us a jar of flowers. There's yellow daisies, a red rose or two, and a few purple lilacs. Then with Ella leading, we march out the door and up the street. It's like a parade. Folks come out of the stores to wave and call to us. "You girls look snappy!"

"What lovely bouquets."

"On your way to the cemetery, are you? Must be Ella's birthday activity."

We stomp so stiff and proud, most of the water in our jars sloshes out. I'm afraid the flowers will wilt before we can get them on the graves.

When we get to the cemetery, it doesn't take a lot of hunting to find raggedy looking graves in Potter's Field. We each pick one. Mine belongs to Samuel Boggs. His name is whittled into a small wooden cross. I sit down on the ground beside him.

"Well, Mr. Boggs," I say, "my name is Gertie Larson. I'm gonna spruce things up a bit for you."

I grab a handful of weeds and pull them up. Then I dig out some rocks and toss them away. As I work, I look around. On the other side of a white picket fence is the Methodist Church section. No weeds or rocks there. Only clean mounds with lots and lots of flowers. Three or four of the graves have beautiful marble angels standing guard over them with their wings spread wide. I'm thinking how different the Methodist graves are from the Potter's Field graves when Ella says, "It looks like we're finished. I think we've done a fine job."

The graves we cleaned and decorated with the jars of flowers do look better. That makes me happy. But they still look pitiful. That makes me sad. No beautiful marble angels guarding them. Just rough wooden crosses with the whittled out names of the poor folks who are buried there—folks who couldn't pay for a plot of tended ground, or didn't have family to care for their graves, or didn't belong to a church.

When we get back to Ella's for the birthday cake and ice cream, me and Ella are alone for a minute. I thank her for letting me win at Musical Chairs.

She fluffs her curls and says, "Just remember, Gertie, your birthday party is next Saturday." Then she says, "All things therefore whatsoever ye would that men should dounto you, even so ye also dounto them."

I want to ask her what a "dounto" is, but before I can, her mother drags her away to open her presents. That's when I make up my mind to have a big sister-little sister talk with Mary. Mary's two years older than me. She's bound to know what a "dounto" is.

6

The Golden Rule

I<small>T'S NOT 'TIL BEDTIME</small> that I get a chance to ask Mary what a "dounto" is. She comes into my room to say goodnight. Her brown hair is rolled up and tied with strips of cloth so it will curl overnight. But it never does. Her hair's like Papa's, straight and fine. But she keeps trying.

"Mary, can we talk?" I ask her.

She nods. We hug and jump up onto my bed.

Pauline peeks at us from under her covers across the room. She's prob'ly thinking we'll want her to leave. Like we do sometimes when we're big sister talkin'. I smile and blow her a kiss. She knows she can stay.

Then I ask Mary, "Do you know what a 'dounto' is?"

"I think you mean do unto," she says, taking a breath between the do and the unto. "It's not a thing. It's a verb. Maybe if you tell me how you heard it, I can help you understand it."

So I tell her about Ella letting me win at Musical Chairs and what Ella said when I thanked her.

"Aha!" Mary laughs. "Good old Ella. She's telling you that she let you win the prize at her party and expects you to let her win the prize at your party. It's the Golden Rule. It's from the Bible. It goes something like this, 'Do unto others as you want others to do unto you.' That means you should treat other people the way you want them to treat you. Understand?"

I nod. We hug again. Mary skips up the hall to her room, and I climb into bed.

For a long while I lay there thinking how blest I am to have a big sister like Mary. Mary's gonna be a teacher when she grows up. She'll make a fine one. She helps me when I get stuck on the times tables and goes-intos. Sad to say, I get stuck a lot. Someday I hope to be as good a big sister to Lorraine as Mary is to me. I just hope Lorraine will be better at her numbers. For her sake. And mine.

Then I think of Sammy. I still feel bad about the way I treated him on the footbridge. Even though he was gonna throw me in the ditch, I know Jesus didn't like the way I acted. After all, we're supposed to treat others like we want them to treat us—with kindness.

I scrunch to the edge of my bed, turn on my back, dangle my head over the side, and look out my window. Upside-down the sky's a sheet of black paper poked full of tiny holes. Twinkling through the holes is the glory of heaven.

"Dear God," I whisper, so as not to wake Pauline, "I'm sorry I acted so mean to Sammy Stevens on the footbridge. Please forgive me. If You'll help me find a way to make things right with him, I promise to always do unto others. Amen." Then I flip on my side, wiggle down under the covers, slip off to sleep, and dream I'm trapezing with the circus.

The very next day, my Sammy prayer is answered! I gotta say, my prayers aren't always answered so quick. But looking back, I figure my Sammy prayer was 'specially important. So was God's answer, I was about to find out.

It's Sunday morning. Me and Mary are skipping up Main Street on our way to Sunday School. Who should be sitting on the curb in front of the harness shop but Sammy. Just as we're about to pass by, he looks up. His eyes are red and watery. He looks so pitiful, I have to stop. Besides, I asked God to help me find a way to make things right with Sammy. Maybe this is it.

"You go on without me, Mary," I tell her, "I'll catch up in a minute."

"Gertie, are you sure?" she asks, and throws a I-don't-trust-him look at Sammy.

"I'm sure," I answer.

"Well, all right," she says, and with a wave goodbye, skips on up the street.

I step closer to Sammy. "Hello, Sammy," I say.

He doesn't answer, just drags his sleeve across his drippy nose. All at once, I'm not afraid of him anymore. All at once, I just feel sorry for him. All at once, I know what he needs. Sammy needs a friend. Yes, I want to be his friend. But he needs a more faithful friend than I can ever be. I'm just a little girl. I can't be there every time he needs somebody to help him. But I know Somebody who can.

I step into the street, bunch my dress around my knees, and sit down on the curb beside him. "Sammy," I ask, "do you know who Jesus is?"

"He's God's Son," he says.

"That's right!" I say, "Bet you learned that in church."

Almost every Sunday I see Sammy, his hair slicked down and his face all scrubbed and shiny, hurrying along the street with his papa on their way to the Presbyterian Church. I wonder why he's not on his way there now. From his watery eyes, I figure something bad must have happened with the bratty boys. But I'm not gonna tackle that now, so I just go on with what I'm saying. "Yes, Jesus is God's Son. He's our Friend, too. There's a hymn that goes, '*What a friend we have in Jesus, all our sins and griefs to bear.*' Do you know that hymn, Sammy?"

"Uh huh," he says, and nods his head.

I hear the bell ringing for church, but I can't leave Sammy now. I'm thinking of what Mr. Tannehill says, "When God gives you a chance to share your faith in Jesus, don't fail to. You don't need to use a lot of big words. Just share what's in your heart—what Jesus means to you." I never shared Jesus before. I'm even a little afraid—afraid I won't say the right thing. But if Sammy only knows Jesus as God's Son, that's not enough. Sammy needs to know Jesus as his Friend and Savior, too. So I send up a quick prayer, "Please, God, help me to say the right thing, and please help Sammy's hurt brain to figure it out." Then I keep on goin', "Sammy, Jesus loves you. He wants to be your Friend. He wants to help you when you're feeling sad or when those bratty boys torment you. Sammy," I ask, "do you want Jesus to be your Friend? You know, like we sing in that hymn, 'What A Friend We Have In Jesus?'"

"I do," he says.

Now comes the hard part. 'Bout us being sinners. But I know Sammy needs to hear it. Just like the rest of us do. Just like they teach us in Sunday School. So, I tell him, "Sammy, Jesus wants to be your Savior, too. Do you know what that means?"

He rolls his eyes, blinks a few blinks, and swings his head from side to side.

"Well, Sammy," I tell him, "God says in the Bible we're all sinners. That means we do things we shouldn't. Like those bratty boys teasing and tormenting you. God tells us to love one another, not tease and torment one another. And it's not just the bratty boys who do wrong things. We all do things God tells us not to do. Sometimes we don't do things He tells us to do. I don't know why we act this way, but it's just born in us to sin and fall short of the glory of God, as the Bible puts it." Sammy is staring at me with big, round eyes. I figure he needs more help to figure out what I'm saying. "Or as my Aunt Danny puts it, 'You have to teach little children to share, but you don't have to teach them to be selfish. They know that right from birth.'" Sammy sighs. I keep on going, "But, Sammy, the good news is, if we ask God to forgive us for any bad things we do, He'll forgive us. He even sent His Son, Jesus, to take the punishment we got comin' as sinners. That's what it means in that hymn when we sing, '. . . *all our sins and griefs to bear.*' It's like Jesus took the blame for our sins to save us from being punished so that some day we can be with Him in heaven. That's why He's called 'Savior.' But for Him to be your Savior, Sammy, you have to ask Him to be your Savior, and . . . "

"I want Jesus to be my Savior," Sammy stops me before I can say another word.

"Then, Sammy, let's pray right now and tell Him so. Would you like to do that?"

"I would," he says.

I hold out my hand. Sammy takes it in his own. We bow our heads.

"Dear Jesus," I start, "Sammy loves You . . . You do love Jesus, don't you, Sammy?" I stop praying long enough to ask him. I figure Jesus needs to know.

"I do," says Sammy.

". . . and wants You to be his Friend and Savior," I go on praying. "Please be his Friend and help him when he needs it, and please be his Savior and forgive him for any bad things he's done." I squeeze Sammy's hand. "Sammy, if you want Jesus to come into your heart and be your Friend and Savior, say 'Amen.'"

"Amen," he says.

I know right then, without a doubt, that Jesus is Sammy's Friend and Savior for life. Course there's other things Sammy needs to know—Bible things like being baptized, and doing unto others. But I'm just a little girl. I'll leave all that up to his preacher. For now, it's enough for Sammy to know that Jesus is his Friend and Savior.

That's when I think of one more thing I should tell him. 'Cause it's important. Especially to someone like Sammy. "And Sammy," I say, "some day when you get to heaven, you won't be teased and tormented by those bratty boys ever again. You'll be just as smart as them. Prob'ly smarter. Jesus will see to that." A tear slides down his cheek. It hangs from his chin, like a drop of melted lard hangs from the spout on Mama's measuring cup. Then it falls, pushed off by another tear.

The rays of the morning sun are shining on top of Sammy's copper colored hair. Just like that day on the footbridge. Only now, instead of his hair looking like it's on fire, it looks like it's glowing with a heavenly light, just like the angel in that picture in our Sunday School class.

I never thought of Sammy Stevens looking like an angel with a halo before. But this morning I do. Because he does. Hurt brain and all.

7

From Glad To Sad To Glad Again

THE NEXT MORNING I wake up thinking how wonderful things turned out with Sammy. I have only one problem left. I still have to think up a birthday activity as fun and exciting as Ella's grave decorating; one that'll keep my guests' minds off the circus and on my party. All day I keep thinking and thinking, but when I go to bed that night, I still haven't come up with an idea. Leastwise, not a good one.

Then I wake up Tuesday morning with the best idea I ever had in the whole wide world! For my birthday activity I'll put on a circus of my own! I've been practicing to be a circus star for years. It'll be easy for me to figure out some circus acts. In fact, one's rumbling 'round inside my head now, thanks to Miss Goldbranson.

Just a week or so ago, she told the class, "This year is the one hundred and seventh anniversary of a successful parachute jump from a hot air balloon over France."

Yes sir, a parachute jump will make a fine act for my circus. I'll use Papa's umbrella, and jump from the balcony outside my bedroom.

Other ideas come tumbling, one after the other. Bare back riding on Mr. Hansen's mare, Jennie. (Mr. Hansen raises horses and lets me ride his little mare now and then.) Tightrope walking on the fence behind our restaurant. Trapeze hanging anywhere but in Mrs. Goosley's precious old apple orchard.

Just then Mama comes into the room. She sits down on the edge of my bed. She slips her hand across the covers, lays it on top of mine, and gives it a pat. "Gertie, I have something to tell you." Her forehead's folded in wrinkles. Her shoulders are saggy. I can tell something's bothering her. "For the past two years," she says, "Papa and I've had some expenses we didn't plan on. Like the new stove for the kitchen." She stands up, reaches behind her, grabs her loose apron strings and flips, twists, and tucks them

24

into a bow, and sits back down again. "Then Mr. Kirkoff raised our rent ten dollars a month." She sighs and shakes her head. "And business hasn't been as good since the hotel hired that French cook."

"But, Mama, you never said anything."

She nods. "We didn't want to worry you girls. Anyway, the circus crowds that'll be here those few days can help us get back on our feet." She turns and stares out the window, "But to take advantage of the extra business those crowds will bring, means we'll be much too busy for you to have a birthday party."

"But *Mama!*"

"I know you're disappointed, Gertie, and I'm sorry. But it can't be helped." She stiffens her back like she does when she's tired or something burns on the stove. "You'll have other birthday parties. Now, I've got to get back to the kitchen."

This is the most awful thing that ever happened to me. Not having a birthday party is like not having a birthday at all. Everybody has a party. Except Sammy Stevens, of course. What will my friends say? What will they think? Especially Ella. Birthday parties are very important to Ella. Hers and everybody else's. She's planning to win the prize at my party because she let me win the prize at hers. When she finds out there's no party and no prize, will she still be my best friend?

Later at school, me and Ella are sitting on a bench together. It's recess. I finally worked up how I'm gonna tell her about me not having a party. I'm gonna say I made up my mind not to have a party so I can help more in the restaurant with the circus crowds. I'm gonna say I don't want to cause Mama and Papa the extra work of a party at such a busy time. I'm gonna say when I told Mama I was giving up my party to make things easier on everybody, she cried and cried and said what an unselfish and thoughtful little girl I am.

But before I can tell Ella my story, a couple of bratty boys playing catch nearby keep throwing their ball so it'll bounce our way and hit us on our feet and legs. I soon have my fill of it. I grab the ball and throw it with all my might. It sails up into the air and over the fence. The last we see of it, it's rolling down the middle of Fourth Street.

"Gee whiz, Gingersnaps!" the bratty boy they call Buck whines at me. "What did ya' have to go and do that for? Now we can't play catch anymore. You spoiled our recess. We'll prob'ly get blamed for losing the ball."

He kicks at the dirt. His face is red. And you know what? I'm glad! Just for a minute I know what it feels like to be a bratty boy. And I like it. Just for a minute.

Ella taps me on the shoulder. "Are you through playing ball, 'Gingersnaps?' Can we talk about something important now?"

"Yes," I tell her, and throw her a don't-call-me-Gingersnaps look.

"What time is your birthday party Saturday?" she asks me.

There it is, out in the open. Leave it to Ella to bring it up. But instead of telling her my party story the way I was gonna, my mouth gets dry as summer. I can't say a word. So, I hunch my shoulders, hold them there a second, then drop them down again. Grandma Larson says, "A shrug can say a lot." And it works. Kind of. Ella goes on to something else.

"Well, then, what about your birthday activity?" she asks me.

Since the shoulder thing worked before, kind of, I try it again—hunch them up, hold them there, drop them down again.

"Gertie! Really!" Her curls bounce around sassy-like. I know I'm in for a scolding. "Today is Tuesday. In four days it will be your party, and all you can do is shrug your shoulders? You don't seem to be taking your birthday serious. I am shocked!"

I know right then she won't believe my "unselfish" and "thoughtful" story. I need more time to figure out a better way to tell her. So, I just say, "I am, too, taking it serious. After all, it's my birthday."

"Well, then," she says, "tell me what you have planned for a birthday activity."

I'm hoping recess will end and we'll have to march back to class. But it doesn't. I know I have to do or say something. Since a shrug didn't work before, I look her straight in the eye and tell her, "I'm not ready yet to say what my birthday activity is."

That doesn't work either. She looks straight back at me. "Why not?" she asks. "I'm your best friend. Surely you can tell me."

That's when I think of something I figure will stop her right in her tracks. "Well," I say, "you never told me what your birthday activity was."

She raises her hand with her fingers clenched together, all but the pointer. She sticks the pointer under my nose and wiggles it like a pesky fly. "You never asked me!"

Then she studies me with squinty eyes 'til my head begins to pound like it does when I hang upside-down too long. At last she says, "Why, Gertie Larson, I don't believe you even have a birthday activity!"

I'm not proud of what I say next. Actually, I try to keep the words from coming, but they slip through my lips, smooth and easy. "I do, too, have a birthday activity," I lie. "It's the most specialist birthday activity anybody has ever had."

"Then why . . ." she starts to say.

"I can't tell you yet," I lie some more, "It's . . . ah . . . it's . . . a surprise." I don't know where the "surprise" idea comes from. It sort of piggy-backs on the rest of my made-up story. Lies are like that. Once you start haulin' one around, it most likely will get bigger and heavier.

Ella claps her hands. "I love surprises! Oh, Gertie, I can hardly wait 'til Saturday. I bet you have a fun game planned, too, with a lovely prize for the winner." She waves her eyelashes at me. "Remember how you won the prize at my party?"

I try to stretch my mouth into a smile, but it won't stretch.

"What's the matter?" she asks, "You look sick."

Just then the bell rings. Recess is over at last. I'm glad I don't have to answer any more of her questions. Even so, the rest of the day seems dark and gloomy. By the time Friday rolls around, it still seems dark and gloomy. I figure it's 'cause I lied to Ella and my conscience is poking me. It most likely won't stop 'til I tell her the truth, which I make up my mind to do as soon as I see her. She'll either forgive me. Or she won't. I already asked God to forgive me. And He has. I can tell it here in my heart. Like we learned in Sunday School, God forgives us when we do something bad if we ask Him to forgive us and promise not to do it again. I promised not to lie again.

After breakfast and chores, I'm making my way through the dining room with Mary and Pauline. We're heading for the front door and school. Papa waves for us to stop. "You two go on to school," he tells Mary and Pauline, "I want to talk to Gertie."

Mary looks at me with sad eyes. This morning waitin' tables I dropped a jar of jam and made a mess. Mary's likely thinking Papa's gonna give me the scolding he didn't have time to then. Instead he tells me, "Gertie, someone here wants to meet you." He points to a man sitting at a table by the front window. The man is finishing off a stack of Mama's flapjacks, swimming in melted butter and maple syrup. He grabs his napkin, pulls it across his mouth, and smiles up at me. He has the whitest teeth and the bluest eyes I've ever seen.

Just then, Mama calls Papa into the kitchen. I'm left alone with this smiling customer.

"So, you're Gertie," he says. "Your father's been telling me about your plans to be a trapeze star with the circus when you grow up."

"Yes, sir," I answer.

"He also tells me that tomorrow is your tenth birthday. May I be the first to wish you a happy birthday!" He raises a stiff hand to his forehead in a snappy salute.

That does it. The tears I've been holding back ever since Mama told me I can't have a party, come pouring out of me like water pouring out of the spillway.

"Gertie, what's the matter?" the man asks. "Why are you crying? I thought birthdays were happy affairs."

(Not one person in my family has asked me how I feel 'bout not having a birthday party. Everybody's only thinking 'bout how busy we're gonna be with the circus in town. Now here's somebody I never met before caring enough to ask me why I'm crying.)

It's not like me to tell my problems to someone I just met. But this man makes me think of Grandpa Larson. He has the same kind eyes and friendly smile. I feel like I can talk to him; that he'll listen and understand. And I truly need someone to listen and understand 'cause I'm pretty full up with grief.

So, I give my eyes a quick wipe, and start, "I needed an exciting birthday activity that'd make my party as good as Ella Neil's and her party is a week before mine and always makes my birthday seem dull and she let me win the prize at her party and expects me to let her win the prize at my party and . . ."

"Whoa, Nelly!" he says, "Take a breath!"

I suck in some air and keep going, ". . . and just when I thought of a wonderful birthday activity Mama tells me we'll be too busy with the circus crowds for me to have a party and I lied and told Ella I'm having a party because I'm afraid she won't be my best friend when she finds out I'm not."

"Whew! That's quite a story, Gertie." He takes his chin in his hand and gives it a rub. "Do I understand you right—you haven't told Ella yet that you're not having a party?"

"Yes, sir," I say.

"Hmmmm, you know I just might be able to help you. But first I'd better introduce myself. My name is Charlie Wyngate." He reaches out his hand. I put mine in his and we pump them up and down together. "I'm the advance man for the circus. Since it's because of the circus you can't have a party, I feel somewhat responsible. Besides, a week ago your father kindly let me hang that circus poster in your restaurant window." He points to the big sign with the clown's face peeking through a bunch of red, green, and yellow balloons. "That's when we got to talking about how you want to be a circus performer some day. I'd like to do something to say 'thank you' for your family's kindness to me, including several cups of coffee-on-the-house."

I'm beginning to feel a little better.

"Here's what I'd like to do," he says. "I want to give you four free passes to the circus. That way you can have your party. You can take your guests to the circus."

I'm beginning to feel a lot better.

"Four passes may not be enough to invite all of the friends you'd like," he says, "but you can tell Ella you're having an exclusive party."

"Exclusive?" I ask.

"Yes," he says, "That means only a few special friends are invited. If I have Ella figured right, she'll love that."

"You have her figured right," I say, and hope with all my heart he does.

"I don't have the passes with me. You'll have to come by the ball park tomorrow morning and pick them up." He digs his fingers through his thick hair like he's scratching his thoughts loose. "Let's see, the wagons arrive around ten tonight. The crews will work all night to get ready for our big opening tomorrow morning following the parade. I should be free by, say, nine tomorrow morning. Come by around then. Is it a deal?" He sticks out his hand. I grab it in mine. We pump them up and down again, this time like good friends. The last thing I see as I head out the door is his bright blue eyes and white teeth shining at me.

On my way to school, I make up my mind to use the fifty cents Aunt Danny always gives me for my birthday to buy my guests a root beer and a bag of peanuts. There'll be no cake and ice cream this birthday. Root beer and peanuts will have to do. The only thing missing is a birthday activity. Maybe Ella won't notice, what with the excitement of the circus and all.

I'm glad I didn't say anything about a birthday party to my school friends. Except Ella, of course. With only four passes to the circus, there'll be just enough for me, Ella, Mary, and Pauline. My sisters always come to my parties. I always go to theirs. Along with Ella, they're my best friends. I know some girls at school who don't feel that way 'bout their sisters. Leastwise, they don't act like it. But I figure if God put me and my sisters in the same family, He means for us to get along and love each other. And we do. Most of the time.

Later, after spelling and reading, Miss Goldbranson asks me and Ella to clean the blackboard erasers. We take them outside and 'round to the back of the schoolhouse. There's a couple of scrub oaks there that give a bit of shade. Since we're alone, I figure now is a good time to tell Ella about my birthday party.

"My party will be tomorrow at two o'clock," I say.

(I picked two o'clock 'cause most of the dinner customers will be gone by then. I'm hoping Mama will give me some time off, which I think she will since Aunt Danny and Grandma Larson said they'd help at the restaurant, too.)

Ella smiles. "Tomorrow at two. I can hardly wait."

"We'll meet at the restaurant," I tell her, "but my party won't actually be there."

Ella's eyebrows jump to the top of her forehead and sit there. "What do you mean?"

"Well," I say, "I'm taking my guests to the circus."

Ella stops pounding her erasers. Her cheeks go from peach to red. "How nice," she says. She pats her hair. Little clouds of chalk dust sit on her dark curls. Then, like she just thought it up, she tells me, "Of course, I was going to the circus anyway."

When we finish cleaning the erasers, we head back to the classroom. Just as we get to the door, Ella says, "What I'm really looking forward to is your birthday activity. You did say it's the most specialist birthday activity anyone has ever had."

I should have known Ella'd never forget a birthday activity.

Later, on the way home, I tell her about "exclusive." Mr. Wyngate was right. Ella likes the idea. I tell her about picking up my tickets the next morning from my dear friend who's in charge of the circus. I don't tell her they're free passes.

"Oh, may I come with you?" she asks.

I don't see any harm, so I tell her she can.

In my prayers that night, I thank the Lord Jesus for Charlie Wyngate, the circus, and my free passes. Then I lay in bed a long time too excited to sleep. All at once I hear a rumbling noise. It sounds like thunder. Oh, no, I think, it's gonna rain and spoil everything! The rumbling gets louder, but there's no lightning. Then I figure it out. It's the circus wagons coming!

I crawl out my window onto the balcony. There's only a sliver of moon overhead. I can barely make out the wagons with their drivers clucking giddy-yup noises at their horses. Then somebody hangs a lantern in the General Dry Goods store across the street. In its pale yellow light, the big dark shape of an elephant sways back and forth as it plods up the street behind the wagons.

At last the street is empty and still. I climb back inside my room and slip into bed. My heart is pounding so hard, I'm afraid it'll wake up Pauline.

8

The Surprise!

THE NEXT MORNING ON the way to pick up my free passes, me, Ella, Mary, and Pauline are skipping along Main Street. Pauline starts singing and the rest of us join in. *"A passing policeman found a little child. He walked beside her, dried her tears, and smiled. Said he to her kindly, 'Now you mustn't cry. I will find your mother for you by and by.' Suddenly . . . "* And like the song says, *suddenly* there's Sammy Stevens across the street in front of Doc Summer's office. He's hunched down on the sidewalk. A couple of bratty boys are standing over him.

We stop skipping and singing to see what's going on. One of the bratty boys folds his fingers into a fist and brings it down in the middle of Sammy's back. The other bratty boy does the same. It makes me so mad, I yell at them, "You bratty boys leave Sammy alone!" But they don't stop pounding on him. So I take off across the street waving my arms and shouting, "I'm gonna tell Miss Goldbranson on you! And Mr. Tannehill!" I don't know who scares them off. Prob'ly Miss Goldbranson. They tear up the sidewalk, 'round the corner of the courthouse, and out of sight.

I get down on my knees next to Sammy. His face is wet with tears. I put my hand on his shoulder and give him a pat. "Those bratty boys aren't worth crying over, Sammy," I tell him.

"I'm not crying over those boys, Gertie," he says. He wipes his eyes on his sleeve, and folds his hands under his chin.

I'm afraid he's gonna pray his silly prayer. "Then what are you crying over?"

He says, "I'm crying over Jesus."

I say, "Over Jesus! Why ever are you crying over Jesus?"

He says, "'Cause He didn't come when I called Him."

I say, "He didn't come, Sammy, 'cause He's in heaven."

He says, "But you told me if I called Him, He'd come and help me."

"And He will, Sammy, and He does, and He did," I say.

That's when I think of what Mr. Tannehill told us in Sunday School a week or two ago. If I can tell it to Sammy so he can understand it, I know it'll make him feel better. It did me. "Sammy, when Jesus comes to live in our hearts, He doesn't come in a body of flesh and skin and bones you can see. He comes in a spirit body. That's how He can fit in our hearts and be in heaven at the same time. But even though you couldn't see Him just now when you called Him to help you, He did help you. He sent me. He put it in my mind to run off those bratty boys. They did run, didn't they?"

His head bobs up and down.

"Gertie, are you ever coming?" It's Ella. She sounds grumpy. She doesn't like me spending time on Sammy. 'Cause he's different. 'Cause of his hurt brain.

"Just a minute," I answer. Then, since I can't figure anything else to do for Sammy, I start back across the street. But something makes me stop. I turn and look at him again. He has his hands folded under his chin like before. That's when a voice inside my head whispers, "Do unto others as you would have others do unto you." It's that Golden Rule! And it gives me an idea.

I run back to Sammy. "How would you like to come to my birthday party this afternoon? I'm taking my guests to the circus." I know I have only four passes, and not one of them is for Sammy. But it's Jesus' Golden Rule. I'll leave it up to Him to work things out. All I have to do is trust Him.

"I'd like to come to your party, Gertie." Sammy tells me.

"Really, Gertie!" It's Ella again, sounding even grumpier.

"Sammy," I say, not paying her any mind, "we're on our way to the ballpark to pick up my passes. Would you like to come with us?"

He says he would, and we head back across the street together.

When Ella sees Sammy's red eyes, she throws him a weak smile. Even though she'd never say so, I know she feels sorry for Sammy. There's a lot of good in Ella. It's just not always easy to find.

Then it's up the sidewalk we go. Us girls skipping ahead. Sammy loping behind.

When we get to the ballpark, it's not the same old dusty diamond we're used to seeing. It's way different now! There're side shows lined up along first and third baselines. Pictures of strange looking circus folks are painted on the canvas fronts. One's of a man who weighs over four hundred pounds! Another's of a lady with a long silky beard! In left and right fields are the food booths. Popcorn! Peanuts! Hot dogs! Root beer! Cotton candy! I can smell the hot dogs and popcorn cooking now. It makes my stomach grumble. In the middle of center field is the Big Tent. That's where acrobats will do somersaults; clowns will toss buckets of water—not water, actually, but tiny bits of blue paper that screaming and ducking folks will think is water—and trapeze stars will soar through the air like giant white birds. Oh, the wonder of it all! The wonder of it all!

I tell the others to wait for me by home plate while I look for my friend, Charlie Wyngate. I don't want Ella with me when he gives me my free passes. I know if she finds out they're free, she'll make something out of it, and it won't be something good.

It doesn't take me long to find Mr. Wyngate. He's leaning against a wagon with a picture of a man twisted into the shape of a pretzel painted on the side. "Gertie girl," he says when he sees me, "I was afraid you wouldn't come." He laughs. I know he's teasing me. Friendly like. Not like the bratty boys tease.

While he's talking, Ella, Mary, Pauline and Sammy don't stay put at home plate like I told them to. They follow me and stand a ways off. I figure it's Ella's doing. She always has to be in on everything.

Mr. Wyngate looks over at them. "I see you brought your birthday guests with you. Say, who's the big fellow? He looks a bit rumpled."

"That's my friend, Sammy Stevens," I tell him. "He's been crying. The bratty boys were tormenting him again because of his hurt brain. It makes him feel bad when somebody treats him mean 'cause of something he can't help."

Mr. Wyngate blows out a long sigh. "Yes, I know. Some folks can be thoughtless, even cruel, to someone with a special problem. Someone different from them. And the hurt can go very deep." He takes four passes from his pocket and hands them to me. "Looks like you need five now instead of four."

"Well, yes sir, I guess I do," I say.

Mr. Wyngate reaches in his back pocket, pulls out a little black book, and scribbles on one of the pages. Then he tears it out and hands it to me. "Give this to the man in the ticket booth when you come this afternoon." On the page it says, *This is my special friend, Sammy. Admit him to the circus as my guest. C. W.*

Happiness rises in my throat like the sweet repeat of Mama's tapioca pudding. "Yes sir, thank you, Mr. Wyngate!" I say.

Mr. Wyngate gives me a salute like he did at the restaurant. With all this saluting, I wonder if he was ever in the Army. Then he turns and walks away. That's when I see for the first time that one of his shoes has a lot thicker sole than the other. With each step he takes, his whole body rocks back and forth. All at once, he stops and looks at Sammy. I know he's looking at Sammy 'cause his sad face says so.

"Gertie, come here a minute," he calls to me.

When I'm standing close beside him, he asks me a question that makes my knees wobble. "How would you and your guests like to ride Jumbo the elephant in the circus parade this morning?"

"Yes, sir, thank you, sir, Mr. Wyngate, sir!" I tell him.

"Then it's a deal," he says. He sticks out his hand, but not for me to grab. He lays it on my head and swishes my hair around a bit. In a friendly way.

I turn and race back to the others. I can hardly wait to see their happy faces when I tell them the wonderful news!

"Well," I say, "now I can tell you what my surprise birthday activity is!"

Ella's curls begin to shake. She flips her head to one side. "Well, don't just stand there grinning, Gertie, tell us what it is!"

I fold my arms across my chest like the trapeze stars do when they march proud as peacocks into the Big Tent. "We're riding Jumbo the elephant in the circus parade!"

But the happy faces I was sure I'd see, plainly aren't there. Ella sucks in a big gulp and grabs at her throat. Mary turns white as a sheet. Pauline makes little pitiful noises. And Sammy? He's the only one stretching his mouth so wide, you can count every tooth in his head.

9

The Parade!

STARING UP AT JUMBO's gray wrinkled body is like staring up at the Richfield Court House. Both are big and tall. 'Cept the Court House is painted white. And it isn't wrinkled.

It's easy to see why Mary, Pauline, and Ella were afraid when I told them 'bout riding Jumbo in the parade. They most likely were thinking how scary he'd be up close. And he is. It's one thing to see him plodding up Main Street in the lamplight from the General Dry Goods store, or doin' his tricks yards and yards across the sawdust floor of the circus tent. It's another thing to be standing by him now, close enough to touch him.

Mary whispers in my ear, "Now I know how the barbarians felt the first time they saw the Great Wall of China." Mary'll make a fine teacher some day.

All around us acrobats are practicing cartwheels and back flips. Clowns with painted faces are bouncing bunches of balloons off each other's head. Tigers and lions are roaring, and monkeys chattering in their cages. In the middle of all the rumble and jumble, Mr. Wyngate comes dragging a ladder and leans it against Jumbo's lumpy side.

"All right, Gertie girl," he tells me, "since it's your birthday, you may ride on Jumbo's head."

I feel like I'm gonna be sick.

Mr. Wyngate takes my hand and boosts me onto the lower rung of the ladder. Just for a minute I want to shake his hand loose and run for home. But I prayed for a birthday activity as exciting as Ella's grave decorating. If this is God's answer, I gotta show Him I trust Him no matter how scared I am. So, up, up, up I climb.

When I get to the top, I slide onto Jumbo's head, slip my right leg behind his right ear, and hang my left leg over his forehead. Then I grit my teeth and hunch my shoulders. Like I do when I try not to step on a bug.

Pauline climbs the ladder next onto Jumbo's back. She wraps her arms 'round my waist and hugs me tight. "Gertie, I'm scared," she whispers. I want to tell her not to be scared. But I can't. My lips are frozen.

Next comes Ella. She looks like she's got a bad toothache. Then comes Mary. She doesn't look too good either. Last comes Sammy. His eyes are sparkly, and he's still grinning for all he's worth.

Mr. Wyngate's standing below with a man dressed in a blue and gold uniform. "Children," he calls up to us, "this is Hal, Jumbo's trainer. He'll guide Jumbo in the parade." Then he slowly climbs the ladder. I can hear his thick soled shoe scraping against the rungs. His bad foot may slow him down, I say to myself, but it surely doesn't stop him in his tracks.

"While we're waiting, I thought you'd like to know something about Jumbo," he tells us. "Jumbo's an Asian elephant. He's ten and a half feet tall and weighs eleven thousand pounds. He's fifteen years old and could live as long as sixty years."

"Oooooo," says Pauline, "that's almost as old as Grandma Larson."

A shiny black horse in a harness covered with sparkles is pulling a calliope into place ahead of us. I remember Miss Goldbranson telling us once that a calliope is a steam organ played on a keyboard like a piano. "It has little pipes that the music whistles out of," she said. Miss Goldbranson knows a lot about music. Her father plays a drum in the Richfield Marching Band.

"Jumbo's ears are big to help keep him cool," Mr. Wyngate is saying. "Each ear has many blood vessels. When Jumbo is too warm, he flaps his ears. The air cools the blood vessels, and this cools Jumbo."

With my right leg behind Jumbo's right ear, this is not good news to me.

A man in a white suit with lots of gold trim, climbs onto the calliope. "Looks like we're about to start," says Mr. Wyngate. He reaches in his back pocket, pulls out a bundle of small American flags, and gives one to each of us. "Oh, and one more thing," he says, "you may have heard that elephants are moody and can be dangerous, some even running amuck and trampling people. But don't worry. Jumbo's very gentle. Now, have a good time, and don't forget to wave your flags." He slowly backs down the ladder to the ground. Then he lifts the ladder and hauls it away.

I think of what Grandma Larson says, "The die is cast." Actually, it means you're stuck. That's how I'm feeling now—stuck on Jumbo's big bony head.

The man in the calliope flips the back of his fancy coat out of the way, and slides onto a bench. The lively notes of a Sousa march begin whistling through the steam pipes. The calliope moves slowly onto Main Street with us next behind it.

Just then, I think of something—something the tigers, lions, monkeys, clowns, and Jumbo—mostly Jumbo—made me forget. Me, Mary, and Pauline are supposed to be back at the restaurant by now helping with the morning rush. Mama let us go to the ballpark to pick up my passes only after we promised to come right back and help. Course it shouldn't be too busy now, I figure. Lorraine will be taking her morning nap. Everybody in town will be out on the sidewalk watching the parade. But that means Mama, too! What will she think when she sees Jumbo parading by with us hanging onto his back for dear life?

Up ahead, I see Mrs. Goosley standing on the corner. I think of how I hoped to have my birthday activity in her precious old orchard 'til she ran me off in a most unfriendly way. Course if she hadn't, we wouldn't be riding Jumbo now. Makes me think of that Bible verse, "No matter how bad things get, God can make something good out of 'em, if you love and belong to Him." Or words kinda like that.

"Yoo-hoo, Gertie!" It's Mrs. Goosley yelling and waving her handkerchief at me.

I look the other way. Why should I wave back at her after the way she treated me? No, I'll pay her no mind. Serves her right.

That's when it happens. That's when Jumbo tries to shake us loose!

All at once, he starts dipping and swaying and stomping for all he's worth! He swings his head from side to side with me swinging along! I grab for something to hang onto, and come up with a handful of elephant ear.

Mr. Wyngate's words, "dangerous," "running amuck," and "trampling people" beat like a drum inside my brain. I don't just feel like I'm gonna be sick. I am sick.

Pauline is sobbing against my back. I twist 'round and look at Mary and Ella. They're wrapped in each other's arms, their eyes squished shut. Behind them Sammy's bouncing this way and that way on Jumbo's backside. And he's smiling and waving his flag. *Smiling and waving his flag!*

"This is fun," he yells, "Jumbo's dancing!"

I look down at the trainer. Sure enough, Hal's poking Jumbo on his knee with a stick! With each poke, Jumbo stomps a big foot onto the ground and sways back and forth in time with the music.

It's a long while before I can swallow.

"Yoo-hoo, Gertie!" It's Mrs. Goosley again, yelling and waving her handkerchief.

This time I wave my flag at her. I don't feel so mad at her anymore. She seems friendly enough. Maybe if I treat her the same—like a friend—she'll let me pick an apple now and then. If I ask her first. It's worth a try, I figure, and I wave my flag at her again.

Jumbo's plodding along nice and easy now. I don't feel scared anymore. Leastwise, not as scared as I did.

The sidewalk's full of folks laughing and waving. I see Ella's papa and mama up ahead standing in front of the funeral parlor. Mrs. Neil is on her tippytoes so she won't miss anything. She's smiling and fluttering her fingers in a dainty wave. Then she sees Ella. She throws an arm across her eyes and falls back against Mr. Neil. He catches her and drags her into the parlor. She's not smiling and waving as she goes.

Halfway up the block there's Papa talking to Sammy's father and to my friend, Mr. Hansen. I'm afraid when Papa sees us riding in the parade, and not at the restaurant helping, he'll be awful mad. But when he sees us, he doesn't look awful mad, he looks awful glad. He grabs Mr. Stevens' arm and points up at Sammy. When Mr. Stevens sees Sammy, he doesn't look awful glad, he looks awful mad. Then Papa and Mr. Hansen put an arm around his shoulders, bend their heads close to his, and start talking to him for all they're worth. Before you know it, the three of them are laughing and pounding each other on the back. Just like the bratty boys.

Mr. Stevens cups his hands around his mouth and calls, "Hello, Sammy! Hello, son!"

I look back at Sammy. His face is all shiny like sunbeams are peeking through it.

But the sun isn't out for long. A few doors up the street, there stands Mama and Aunt Danny on the restaurant balcony. Mama is clutching the railing. Her face is red. Her back is stiff. Her eyes are staring. At us! It looks like stormy weather ahead for the Larson sisters. Pauline and Mary must see her, too. Pauline's arms get tighter around my middle, and Mary calls out, "Oh, oh!"

Just as we get in front of the restaurant, Mama leans over the railing, wags her finger at us, and opens her mouth like she's gonna yell something. But before she can get the yellin' done, Aunt Danny waves her apron at me and shouts, *"Happy Birthday, Gertie!"*

That's when something happens, something you'd never dream of or think to wish or pray for—something that makes this birthday activity the best real life adventure in the whole wide world! Up and down the street, neighbors and friends, even strangers, join in. *"Happy Birthday, Gertie! Happy Birthday, Gertie! Happy Birthday, Gertie!"*

When the man in the calliope hears all the shoutin', he stops his Sousa march in the middle of a chord, and swings into "For He's A Jolly Good Fellow."

The bratty boys are standing on the sidewalk watching. Their mouths are hanging open. I want to yell, "Nyah nyah nyah nyah nyah." But my heart is so full of joy, I smile and wave my flag at them instead. Anyway, I promised God to always do unto others. And you know what? It works! The bratty boys smile and wave back. Maybe like Ella there's good in them after all. Though to be honest, I doubt it.

As the music and cheering go on and on, even Mama joins in. Then someone pats me on the shoulder. It's Ella. Her eyes are sparkly.

"This is the most specialist birthday activity anyone has ever had!" she shouts above the noise.

I never thought I'd ever hear those words from Ella. Not about anybody else's birthday activity. I feel like I'm floating on a pink cloud of cotton candy.

I look back up Main Street to where the parade started. Flags are waving from the top of the circus tent. They seem to be waving at me. Me, Gertie Larson, who wasn't even supposed to have a birthday party. Me, Gertie Larson, who scrapes and scrubs . . .

I feel a jab in my ribs. It's Ella again. Her eyes are squinty.

"I can hardly wait 'til your birthday party next year," she yells. "You'll certainly want a birthday activity *at least* as exciting as this one."

Now, you're prob'ly thinking, I bet Gertie feels like she's gonna be sick. But I don't. 'Cause I'm too happy. God gave me this wonderful birthday activity. Nothing is gonna spoil it for me. Not even my best friend, Ella Neil.

10

The Life In Real Life Adventures

FOR A COUPLE OF weeks after my birthday, as I went about my daily doings—tending Lorraine, scrubbing dishes, practicing trapezing— I'd stop and rest and think about my wonderful birthday party. It's kinda like that word in the Bible, "Selah."

Mr. Tannehill told us in Sunday School, "Selah is a Hebrew word that means stop and rest. It's found mostly in the Book of Psalms. It was put there to remind the musicians and singers to pause and get their breath. But," and he sucked in a big breath of his own, "I believe Selah has a spiritual application, too. I believe God put it in the Bible to teach us to stop and rest so we can think more deeply about what He's saying to us in His Word. Selah."

So I was doing a lot of stopping, resting, and thinking—Selahing— and a little bit of worrying, too. I was worrying about what Ella said, that I'll have to think up something at least as exciting as riding Jumbo for my birthday activity next year. I know it was just Ella talking. But I know she's right. If I've learned one thing from Ella, it's that a good party giver makes sure each party is at least as good as the one before it. If not better.

I learned, too, but not from Ella, that The Golden Rule really works. When you do unto others, they'll do unto you, too. Course you gotta be careful when you do unto a bratty boy 'cause you never know what he'll do unto you back. And I learned that a real life adventure doesn't have to be big and exciting, like riding an elephant in a circus parade. One of the biggest and best real life adventures happens when you're kind to somebody and somebody's kind to you.

Yes sir, I learned that it's the *life* in a real life adventure that's the best part. Even better than the *adventure* part. You'll see what I mean in a poem I wrote for you. Actually, I had to write it for Miss Goldbranson. At first, I didn't know what to write or how to write it. Poetry is tricky.

The words at the end of the lines have to sound sorta alike. I sat there for a long time staring at my empty piece of paper. Then Ella leaned across the aisle and stuck her paper under my nose to show me what she was writing. The name of her poem was "Things." It started, "Getting things is what life is all about. Doing things is what makes me laugh and shout." Her poem gave me the idea for my poem. I call it, "The Life in Real Life Adventures." I hope you like it. Miss Goldbranson did. Wait 'til you see what she wrote at the end!

The Life In Real Life Adventures
By Gertie Larson

Life is not things.
I've learned it is true
That life is what happens
Between me and you.

Life is relationships,
Friendships with others.
It's treating all people
Like sisters and brothers.

So whether at home
Or at church or at school,
To live a good life
Live by God's Golden Rule.
Selah.

"Gertie—Your poem is lovely and deserves an 'A.' If memory serves me, this is the first 'A' you ever earned in my class. Congratulations! I showed your poem to Editor Richards. He's considering publishing it in the 'Poet's Corner' of *The Richfield Reaper*. Again, congratulations! Miss Goldbranson"

There's one more thing I want to share with you. It's about what I wrote in the last line in my poem, "Live by God's Golden Rule."

Sad to say, it's not always easy to live by God's Golden Rule. Like when somebody's mean to you, it's not always easy to do unto them like you wish they'd done unto you—like be nice to you instead of mean. Remember those bratty boys who kept hitting me and Ella with the ball at recess that day? And how I grabbed the ball and threw it over the fence? Well, I didn't follow God's Golden Rule that day. I didn't treat those bratty boys like I wished they'd treated me. But I've learned in Sunday School that if I really try, Jesus will help me do good unto others even when others do mean unto me. All because I asked Him to come and live in my heart.

That's what Sammy did, too, remember? Once Sammy had Jesus in his heart, his life got better. Like folks used to have little to do with him. Some were even afraid of him. Me for one. But not any more because now Sammy has Jesus in his heart. Now he isn't the mean old Sammy I met on the footbridge that day, jabbing his fists in the air, and yelling, "I'm gonna throw you in the ditch!" Now he's the smiling, flag waving Sammy folks saw riding on Jumbo in the circus parade—leastwise, most of the time he is. Now folks treat him like any other child—leastwise, most of the time they do. Now Sammy's happier. Folks are happier, too. All because of Jesus.

Yes sir, having Jesus as your Friend and Savior is the best real life adventure in the whole wide world! Just ask Sammy. He'll tell you. Hurt brain and all.

Well, this ends my first real life adventure. But remember, there's a second one comin' along. And it's got Indians in it!

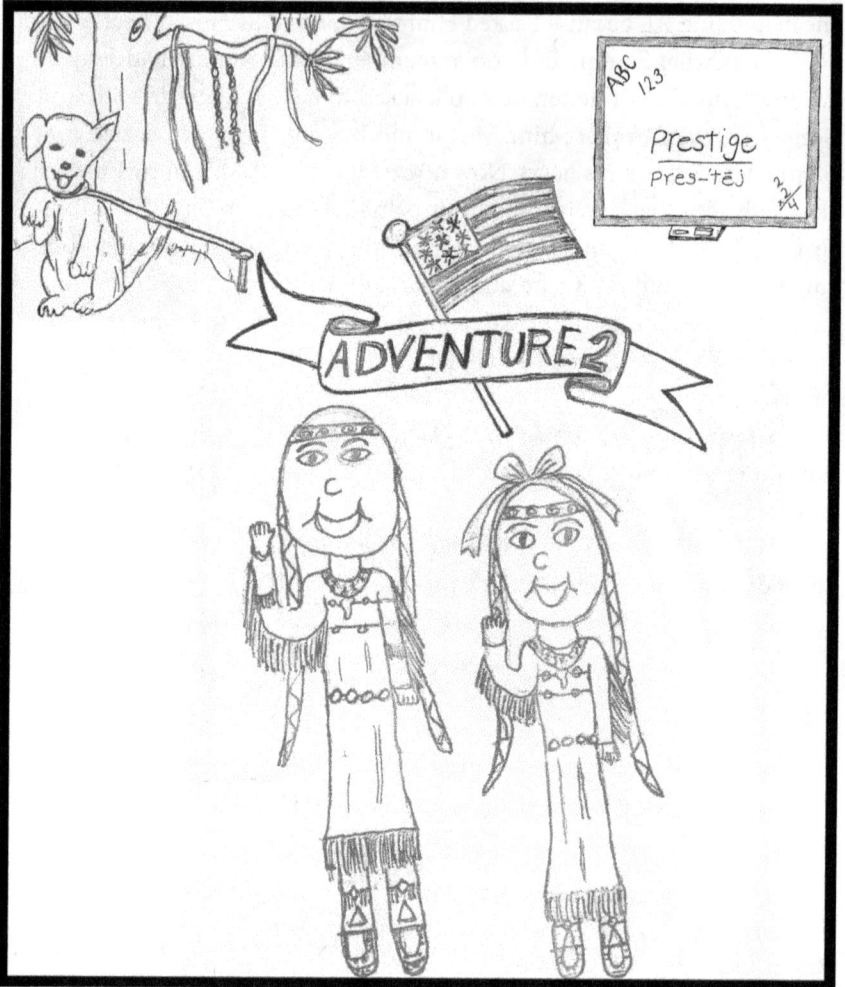

11

Gulpin' and Gaspin'

Sometimes real life adventures come in bunches. You barely get done with one when another one pops up. That's what happened with my next real life adventure. My first one was barely over when the second one came knockin' at my door.

It started last Halloween, which most folks say was Richfield's wildest and woolliest ever. More windows were soaped 'round town than you could shake a stick at. The windows in my family's restaurant got their share and then some. I watched Papa scrape the soap off for hours.

Actually, soaped-up windows was the least of the tricks 'round town. Like Preacher Jones of the Methodist Church came running down the middle of Main Street. He was flapping his arms and hollering for help to round-up the cows somebody herded into his sanctuary. It took lots of scrubbing and airing out before preaching, praising, and praying were heard inside its doors again. Mr. Dinwiddie and his two brothers had to borrow the Volunteer Firemen's hook and ladder to climb to the top of the courthouse. His wagon was up there. A trickster had taken it apart, hauled it piece by piece to the courthouse roof, and put it together again. Every outhouse in town was tipped over. (This of all the tricks caused the most commotion.) Somebody dumped a crate of live chickens in the spillway. Sad to say, the crate didn't float and the chickens couldn't swim. And Widow Gustafson's little children were scared out of their wits when a couple of sheet covered goblins floated out of the night and pounded on their bedroom window. The goblins got the worst of the bargain though. Spunky Widow Gustafson doused them with a bucket of icy water.

"I told you, Ella, we shouldn't pick on Widow Gustafson's little children. I told you . . ."

"Oh, Gertie, stop your gulping and gasping and wring out your sheet."

It took about a week for the town to clean-up the soapy windows, right the tipped-over outhouses, round-up the lost cows, bury the drowned chickens, and take care of all the other Halloween leftovers. It's Sunday now. Me and Ella are sitting side by side in Mr. Tannehill's Sunday School class.

"Good morning, children," he tells us. "Let's bow our heads and open in prayer."

He starts off praying like he does every Sunday. But instead of stopping after a minute or two, he keeps on going and going, thanking God for this and thanking God for that. I get a bad feeling he's building up to something. Sure enough, when he finally gets to the end he says, "Children, I have some exciting news. We're going to put on a Thanksgiving program this year. Everyone in town is invited to attend." He looks kinda puffed up, strutting back and forth in front of the class. I figure the program must be his idea. "Miss Goldbranson is co-sponsoring the event with me." As he says her name, he shows lots of gum and teeth. He always does.

Just a month ago, Mr. Tannehill and Miss Goldbranson got promised to be married. They make a handsome couple, except both have bushy eyebrows. Hers are like golden, feathery butterfly wings. His are like dark, furry caterpillars laid out across his forehead. Makes him look like he's peeking out from under a hedge.

Mr. Tannehill's saying, "You who are in Miss Goldbranson's fifth grade class will be hearing more about the program in the weeks ahead."

This means me and Ella. It's all Ella can talk about on our way home after Sunday School. "I wonder what kind of program they're planning? I wonder if there'll be acting parts?" Ella wants to be a famous actress when she grows up.

She finally gets off the program and onto something worth talkin' about. "I heard there's Utes camped north of town."

"Utes!" I say, "Really? Why ever didn't you tell me before?"

"Well, with the excitement of the program and all, I forgot," she says.

That's Ella all right. She's the only one I know who gets more excited about a program than about Indians.

When we get to the funeral parlor, we hug goodbye, and I take off for the restaurant. I go 'bout half a block when I see Sammy Stevens up ahead, bouncing along, part skip, part hop. He keeps opening his sweater and peeking at something he's cuddling next to his middle. If I wasn't so hungry, I'd take out after him to see what he's hauling. But I know Mama's got the customers' dinner ready. I'm hoping there'll be lots of leftovers. So I keep headin' for the restaurant. Anyway, I figure I can find Sammy any time I want. He doesn't wander far. You know, because of his hurt brain and all. Sure enough, the next morning I find him without even trying.

When I get to school Monday morning, a dozen or so children are huddled around something in the school yard. I can't tell what. The ornery bratty boys are laughing and pounding each other on the back, which isn't a good sign. All at once the children move apart, just enough for me to see what they're staring at. It's Sammy. His face is red as his hair. His eyes are watery. He looks pitiful.

"Let me through," I say, elbowing my way between Penny Peterson and the Teeter twins. "Why are you all staring and laughing at Sammy?"

"Look what he's got," one of the bratty boys says. He grabs a handful of Sammy's sweater and pulls it open. A tiny tan face stares out at me. So, that's what Sammy was hauling yesterday, I say to myself. "Well," I ask, "what's so funny about that? Haven't you ever seen a puppy before?"

"We're not laughing at the puppy," the bratty boy says, "We're laughing at what Sammy's named him."

I turn to Sammy. "What have you named your puppy, Sammy?"

His shoulders sag as he looks 'round at all the grinning faces—except mine, of course. I never laugh at Sammy. I don't think being thirteen with the brain of a six-year-old is funny.

At last, he blows out a big sigh and tells me, "Jumbo."

I don't have to ask why he named him that. Riding Jumbo the elephant in the circus parade wasn't only my biggest real life adventure. It was Sammy's biggest real life adventure, too. Of course, Rex or Fido or Rover might fit his puppy better.

I'm wondering where Sammy got Jumbo. I figure he prob'ly found him. Once in awhile a litter of stray kittens or puppies is left in the vacant field in back of the courthouse. I bet he found him there. How else would someone like Sammy get a puppy?

Before I can ask him, the bell rings for class. As we march up the steps, I look back. There stands Sammy all alone in the school yard with Jumbo poking out of his sweater. I get that pain in my chest I get when I think of Sammy not being able to do a lot of the things other children do, like go to school. But at least he has a puppy now; something to love and keep him company while we're on the inside doing and learning things. And he's on the outside peekin' in.

When we're in our seats, Miss Goldbranson starts talking about the Thanksgiving program. "As our class's part of the program, you will each compose an essay on 'What I Have To Be Thankful For.' Mr. Richards, editor of *The Richfield Reaper,* has graciously consented to choose five of the essays—one first place winner, four runners-up—to be read aloud by their authors or authoresses." She studies her fingernails, important-like. "The program will be held in the Fellowship Hall of the Baptist Church the night before Thanksgiving. Following the program, we will enjoy a pie sociable!" Her eyes jump around the room looking for happy faces. She doesn't find one on me.

I feel awful. Even when she says there'll be a five dollar cash prize for the best essay, I still feel awful. I don't like to write. In the first place, I'm not good at it. I only got an "A" once, and that was for a poem. Remember? In the second place, I don't have a lot of fancy clothes or jewels or toys to brag about like Ella. I do have a wonderful family. I'm thankful for that. But I don't figure I can fill enough pages writing about my mama and papa, grandparents, sisters, and an aunt to please Miss Goldbranson. Leastwise, not enough to get an "A". Or to win the contest and the five dollar cash prize.

I look across the aisle at Ella. She's grinning for all she's worth. Which doesn't surprise me. I can almost hear her brain counting up the millions of things she has to be thankful for—a closet full of store-bought dresses, trips on the Denver and Rio Grande to Salt Lake City, practically no chores, naturally curly hair, no freckles, being an only child, parents who never tell her "No," and on and on.

She's bound to win the five dollar cash prize, I figure. She might as well add that to her Thankful List, too.

12

Brawa

THE FIRST THING I do when I wake up Tuesday morning is say a thank you prayer. Not for the "What I Have To Be Thankful For" essay contest. For Sammy's puppy. God likes good manners. If you don't thank Him when He sends a blessing, you most likely will have to wait awhile before another one comes along. I learned that in Sunday School.

I jump out of bed, dress, and hop down the stairs two at a time. I want to get to school. Maybe Sammy'll bring his puppy again. Maybe he'll let me hold him.

After breakfast, Mary and Pauline fill the salt and pepper shakers, and head out the door for school. I start to change my baby sister, Lorraine. Before I can get the wet diaper off and the dry diaper on, there's a knock at the back door.

"Gertie, see who that is," Mama tells me, "Lorraine can wait a minute."

When I open the door, there stands an Indian woman and a little girl. They're dressed like all the other Indians we see about this time each year—trousers or dresses and shoes made of some kind of animal skins, with lots of beads stitched here and there, and fringe on the skirts and sleeves. This mother and her little girl have long, shiny black braids. With their smooth brown skin and big dark eyes, they make a pretty picture. Like in the history books at school. I figure they're with the band of Utes camped north of town. The ones Ella told me about.

The woman pokes a sack at me through the open door. "Brawa," she says.

"Brawa" is the Indian word for flour. Like all the other Indian women who come to our back door, she's hoping we'll scoop some flour into her sack. I asked Mama once why they do this. "It's because they lead a hard life," she said. "Giving them a scoop or two of flour is the least we can do, considering." She never told me what "considering" meant, but she seems to think we owe the Indians the flour. So, I head for the pantry.

Before I can get there, the little Ute girl starts to cough and cough and cough. I never heard anyone cough and struggle for breath so hard before. I turn and look at her. For the first time I see how thin and little she is. She looks about Pauline's age, six, maybe seven.

"Gertie," Mama says, "you'd better go on to school or you'll be late. I'll take care of the flour, and Lorraine."

All day at school, I keep wondering what happened in our kitchen after I left. I can't keep my mind on the lessons.

Miss Goldbranson tells me, "I don't know where your mind is today, Gertie. It's certainly not in this classroom. Go to the blackboard, again, and write the same sentence I had you write earlier. This time do it five times: *A wandering mind is the very worst kind.*"

"Yes, ma'am," I say, and head for the blackboard.

When school is over, I hurry home even though I know chores are waiting. I'm anxious to find out what happened with the little Ute girl.

Mama's at the stove. Steam is floating up from three big pots. It smells so good, my stomach grumbles.

"Mama, what's wrong with that little Ute girl?" I ask.

"I don't know, but I'm afraid she's a mighty sick little girl." She dips a big wooden spoon into one of the pots, blows a cooling breath on it, sucks the golden broth into her mouth, and rolls it around on her tongue. Then she reaches for the salt and pepper shakers. "I told the mother about flour and mustard plasters," she goes on, "even put a drop of coal oil on some sugar cubes for the little girl to suck on for her cough. But I don't know if she'll give them to her or not. She said they're leaving next week for their village; that the medicine man will look after Little Moon Wind when they get there."

Little Moon Wind, Little Moon Wind, Little Moon Wind, I say the words over and over to myself. I never heard such a beautiful name before, 'though it's news to me there's wind on the moon.

That night I lay in bed a long time looking out my window. I can still see Little Moon Wind's skinny body bent double from her awful coughing. I think of her sleeping somewhere in a teepee, most likely on the hard, cold ground, while here we are safe, warm and well in our beds. Maybe that's what Mama meant when she said that giving the Indians a scoop of flour was the least we could do, "considering."

I close my eyes and whisper a prayer so as not to wake Pauline in bed across the room. "Lord Jesus, please help Little Moon Wind get well. And please, Lord, I'd like to be her friend. Amen." Then I go to sleep and dream about elephants and puppies.

The next day at school we have a visitor. He's tall, heavy and has rosy red cheeks. He's standing beside Miss Goldbranson in front of the class.

"Children," Miss Goldbranson says, smiling, and waving her eyelashes, "I'm sure most of you know Mr. Richards, editor of *The Richfield Reaper*. He has kindly consented to address us this morning relative to the upcoming Thanksgiving essay contest. Let's give him a big fifth grade welcome." Which we do, us girls daintily clapping our hands; the boys stomping their feet.

"Good morning, good morning!" Mr. Richards booms in a voice as big and heavy as he is. "How many of you children have begun your Thanksgiving essay?"

Only Ella sticks her arm up and wiggles her fingers.

"My, my," he says, "we certainly need to get busy. That's exactly why I'm here this morning, to make certain we do just that." His spectacles have worked their way down to the tip of his nose. He pushes them back with his thumb. "We're hoping our Thanksgiving program will become one of Richfield's most prestigious annual events."

A couple of bratty boys at the back of the room groan. I'm happy to hear I'm not the only one who wishes the Thanksgiving program had never been thought up. No matter how prestigious it's gonna be.

It takes Mr. Richards 'bout ten minutes to get done with his "need to get busy" talk. Then he heads out the door. After he's gone, Miss Goldbrandson strolls up and down the aisles laying a piece of paper on our desks. So we can work on our essays.

After a bit, I raise my hand and wave so she'll see me.

"Yes, Gertie?" she says.

"Does 'prestigious' mean the same thing as 'prestige'?" I ask her.

Miss Goldbranson fluffs the lace doodad on the front of her blouse and smiles. Like she's pleased with my question. She twirls 'round, steps up to the blackboard and takes a piece of chalk in her hand. She writes both words, prestigious and prestige, on the blackboard, and adds those funny slashes and dashes that tell you how to sound out the word. Then she drags the chalk along under the word prestigious.

"Prestigious is an adjective which in a sentence describes a noun. While prestige," again she drags the chalk along, this time under the word prestige, "is a noun which in a sentence is the name of a person, place, or thing." She smiles again and pokes a wispy strand of hair behind her ear. "Both words are used to express a sense of respect, renown, importance." As she talks, she walks up the aisle to my desk and looks down at my paper. It's empty. She flutters her butterfly eyebrows. "Why did you want to know, Gertie?"

I raise my shoulders up and drop them down again. "I was just wondering."

She sucks in some air, bites down on her lower lip, whirls and strides back down the aisle, all the while poking at the bun of hair bobbing on the back of her neck. Somebody behind me snickers. I don't need to look. I know it's a bratty boy. Later, when it's time to pick somebody to clean the blackboard, I don't need to guess who it'll be. I know it'll be me.

Actually, I don't care. What I learned about prestige that day makes cleaning the blackboard worth it. I learned that some of the people you least expect to have it, have it. Like my mama and papa. They work hard every day so folks will have a nice place to get a bite to eat for a decent price. Then there's little Moon Wind who coughs and chokes at 'bout every breath. And she never bawls or complains. Leastwise, she never did at our back door. Just coughed and choked. And Sammy Stevens. Yes, I think he has prestige. Lots of it. Look how he loves Jumbo. He takes care of his puppy with what Grandma Larson calls "a gentle hand."

Yes sir, there's lots of good folks here in Richfield who have prestige. When I get the chance, I'm gonna tell them so. If I have folks figured right, they'll be proud and happy to hear it.

13

The *Thing*

I'VE LEARNED THAT A real life adventure can have one, two, or even three little adventures that spark the big one into lightin' up. Little Moon Wind and her mama knockin' at our back door was one of these little sparks.

Another spark happens when me and Ella hike to the abandoned mine in the hills near the spring ditch a mile north of town. It's Ella's idea. 'Though I don't mean to fault her for what happens there, 'cause I'm for goin' to the mine, too. It's where we go to play dress-up, most often after Sunday School. Like today.

As we start out, it's clear and sunny, what Mama calls "an unusually balmy fall day." Only two weeks before Thanksgiving and it's still mostly warm and dry.

As we get near the mine, we pass the spring ditch. Beyond is a trail that winds off to the east and over a small hill. There's a spiral of smoke rising above the hill.

"Bet that's from the Ute campfire," I say. It makes me wonder how Little Moon Wind is doing. I send up a quick prayer for her to be feeling better. (Another thing I learned in Sunday School is that you don't have to kneel by your bed to talk to God. He'll listen no matter where, when, or how you pray. Of course, kneeling by your bed is good.)

"Come on, Gertie," Ella says, and runs the rest of the way up the path and into the mine, with me hurrying to keep up.

There's a big dark room just inside the entrance. On either side are boards nailed over some shaft openings so no one will wander in and get hurt or lost in the mine's many tunnels. The roof overhead is sprinkled with wet spots where rain has trickled through. If it wasn't so damp and gloomy, the mine would be a good place for a birthday activity.

"Wait 'til you see the beads and ribbons I brought," Ella says. She shakes the cigar box she's carrying. "There's pink, blue, green, lavender, and red ribbons. I'll weave the green one into your braid. It'll look pretty in your reddish-gold hair." She lifts the lid and takes out a long bright green ribbon. "You dress up first, Gertie."

Mama let me borrow one of her dresses. I slip it over my head and smooth it down over my own dress. Then I pick two strings of Ella's beads and hang them 'round my neck. Ella finishes me off by weaving the green ribbon into my braid.

"You do look pretty, Gertie," she says, "but I wish you had more color in your face." She pats her own peachy cheeks. "You always look so pale."

Just then I remember Ida Mae Clark's hands the last time I was in her millinery shop to run her some errands. She'd just finished stitching a red rose to the brim of a dress hat. Her hands were all red from the dye. I grab the bonnet with the orange poppies Ella brought for dress-up, and yank off a petal. (I figure Ella won't mind. She has dozens of straws and bonnets.) I work up some spit, wet the petal, and rub it 'round and around on my cheeks.

Ella claps her hands. "Oh, Gertie, it's working! You have pretty orange cheeks." Then she takes the petal and swishes it back and forth across my lips. "Ooooooo," she says when she's done.

I'm wishing I had a mirror so I could see myself, when all at once Ella gets stiff as a board. She sucks in a great gulp of air, and lets out the screamiest scream I ever heard.

"Ella, what's the matter?" I grab her shoulders and shake her hard, but she keeps on screaming. Her eyes are bugged out. She's staring at something behind me. I turn and look. A big, shadowy *thing* is sneakin' through the mine entrance. Its long skinny arms are stretched out like it's comin' to get us. With the bright sunlight behind it, I can't tell if it's a bear or what. I start screaming, too. Ella grabs me 'round my neck. We rock back and forth. Our feet scrape against the dirt floor. Then, with Ella still draped 'round my neck, we twist backwards and fall flat onto the ground. And *the thing* keeps coming! My hand finds a dirt clod and closes 'round it. If I can just get Ella off of me, maybe I can get a bead on *the thing*, hit it with the clod, and scare it away.

"Gertie, it's me," *the thing* is calling.

The thing seems to know me!

I put my hand over Ella's mouth to stop her screaming. Then I push her off to the side and sit up. "Who are you?" I can barely whisper the words.

"It's me, Sammy."

"*Sammy!*" All at once, my voice is back. "*What on earth are you trying to do, scare the wits out of us?*"

All at once, I remember tiny faces peeking out a bedroom window. All at once, I remember icy water soaking through my sheet. I look at Ella. She's grinning. I know she's remembering Halloween night, too. And spunky Widow Gustafson.

"Gertie, Gertie," Sammy moans. His body folds in the middle, and he falls to the ground in a pitiful heap.

It doesn't take much figuring to figure something's awful wrong. I bunch Mama's dress around my legs and kneel on the ground beside him. "Sammy, what's the matter?" I ask.

He grabs a wad of his hair in each hand. With great gulps and sighs, he cries out the terrible words, "Jumbo's gone!"

To see just how terrible Sammy's words are, you need to know how he got Jumbo in the first place. Since I didn't tell you before, I'm gonna digress and tell you now.

("Digress" is one of Miss Goldbranson's fancy words. It means to wander off from what's being talked about. But don't worry. I won't wander long.)

I never got round to asking Sammy where he got Jumbo. I just figured he must have found him. After all, who would give one of their puppies to someone like Sammy?

Then one day, I was running an errand for Miss Ida Mae Clark when I met Widow Gustafson's oldest girl, Emily Rose, in front of the General Dry Goods store. Emily Rose is in my class at school. She told me their dog, Molly, had her first litter of puppies about two months before. They had two puppies left. "Would you like one?" she asked me. I told her, "Yes, I'd like one, but my mama says it wouldn't look good to have a dog in the restaurant. Besides, a dog would eat too many of our leftovers."

That's when it came over me where Sammy must have got his puppy. "Did your mama give Sammy Stevens a puppy?" I asked.

"She surely did," Emily Rose said. "In fact, Sammy was at our house when the puppies were born. Mama made Molly a birthing box with some torn up newspapers in it. Sammy got down on the floor beside the box when the puppies started comin'. Every time a puppy popped out, he clapped his hands." Emily Rose rolled her eyes and smiled. "Mama finally told him he should go home. It was getting late. His papa would be worried. But he didn't want to go. He just sat there kinda humming to the puppies. When Mama saw his tenderness for those little pups, right then and there she promised him one for his very own."

"What did Sammy say?" I asked.

"He didn't say anything, just started to bawl," she told me.

"Then what happened?" I asked.

"Well, Sammy grabbed into the box to get his puppy, but Mama told him he'd have to wait at least six weeks before it could be taken away from its mother," Emily Rose said.

"I suppose he bawled some more?" I asked.

"Not really. His face sort of slumped. He said something about knowing how lonely a little puppy would feel without its mother." Emily Rose shook her head, sad like. "After he went home, Mama told me he hasn't had a mama since he was a little tike."

It's a mystery, when you think about it, how different folks can treat the same person so different. Like some folks call Sammy "crazy." The bratty boys tease and torment him. And Widow Gustafson gives him a puppy. Same Sammy, same brain. Different folks, different hearts.

14

Beads, Ribbons, And War Paint

NOW WE'RE BACK INSIDE the abandoned mine. My wandering is over. Sammy is still in a pitiful heap on the ground. For the first time in the gloomy mine, I see his sweater is missing Jumbo's lump.

"Oh, Sammy, do you mean Jumbo's dead?" I ask.

"No," he answers, and pulls his sleeve across his watery eyes.

"Then, is he sick or hurt?" I ask him.

He shakes his head.

"Well, do you mean he's lost?" I try again.

More head shaking.

"Then, what do you mean?" I wave my hand for him to hurry up and tell me.

His next words send shivers up and down my back. "The Indians got him."

"You mean the Utes?" I ask, "The ones camped over the hill? They got Jumbo?"

His head bobs up and down.

All at once it comes over me like a bucket of icy water just how awful this is. The one thing Sammy ever had of his own to love and love him back has been stole away. A fire flares up inside me that makes my ears tingle.

"Well," I say, "they're not gonna keep him. I'm gonna see to that."

Ella grabs my arm. "Now, wait a minute, Gertie. You're not gonna do anything you shouldn't do, are you? Like go to the Ute camp?"

I shake her arm loose and slip Mama's dress down around my feet. "That's the very thing I am gonna do."

Ella jams her fists onto her hips. "And what makes you think they'll give Jumbo to you?" Her head bounces around like a balloon on a stick in the wind. "They must have wanted him pretty bad to have stole him in the first place."

Of course, she's right. Those Indians won't give Jumbo back to me. I'm just a little girl. But an idea's rumbling around inside my head. What if . . . what if . . . what if I had something to trade for Jumbo!

Ella's cigar box is sitting on the ground. I stare down at it. "If I had something to trade for Jumbo, I bet they'd let me have him. Everybody knows how Indians love to trade."

Ella grabs at her throat. "You don't mean my beautiful ribbons and glass bead necklaces!"

Sammy rolls over on his side moaning, "Jumbo . . . Jumbo . . . Jumbo . . ."

I pick up the cigar box. "Well, Ella, what do you say? Are these few trinkets more important—*more prestigious*—than Sammy's broken heart?"

Sammy stops moaning. It's quiet as a tomb in the mine. After what seems like forever, Ella says, "Gertie Larson, sometimes you upset me so. Oh, all right. Take the stupid 'trinkets' and go get yourself scalped. See if I care."

"Thank you, Ella," I say, and take off toward the light of the mine entrance before she can change her mind.

"Wait!" I hear her running after me. "You still got that dye on your face."

"Good," I say. "They'll think it's war paint and know I mean business."

I'm so mad at the Utes for what they did to Sammy, it's like a giant hand's pushing me down the path from the mine. But by the time I start up the trail to the Ute camp, another giant hand's slowing me down. Fear. I want to turn back. But I keep seeing Sammy rolling on the ground moaning over Jumbo. And that keeps me goin'.

As I stumble along the rocky trail, I worry about what I'll do once I get there. The only Indians I know are Little Moon Wind and her mother. I know they wouldn't steal Jumbo. But maybe they can help me find out who did. Maybe they can help me trade some of Ella's ribbons and beads for Jumbo so I can take him back to Sammy.

All at once, the bushes alongside the trail are shoved aside. Out steps the biggest, scariest looking Indian brave I ever saw! He folds his brown arms across his chest, and stares down at me with eyes as black as coal. It seems like forever that he stands there studying me. I can tell from the wrinkles on his forehead he's wondering 'bout the orange paint on my face. How can I make him see I come in peace?

That's when I think of what Aunt Danny says, "Where there's a will, there's a way." I know I have the will—I want more than anything in the whole wide world to get Jumbo back for Sammy—but do I have the way? I look down at the cigar box in my hands. Can this be the way? I open the lid and hold out the box for him to see the pretty ribbons and beads inside. Then I say only three words, "Little Moon Wind."

It works! He nods his head, and waves his hand for me to follow him. I'm not sure, but I think he smiles at me. Anyway, I'm not so scared anymore as I hurry up the trail behind him.

We're soon at the Ute camp, such as it is. There's a couple of raggedy teepees, three bony horses, a smoky campfire, a few children playing about, and one tired old dog. Over under a shady tree, two women are busy grinding something. Looks like acorns. From their popped open eyes and dropped jaws, I can tell they don't have company often. Leastwise, not a little white girl with orange dye all over her cheeks and lips.

The big brave stops at one of the teepees, lifts the door flap, and points for me to go in. It looks dark inside. But I can't stop now. I promised Sammy I'd bring Jumbo back to him. And I mean to try.

"Thank you, Mr. Indian," I say. Then I call out, "Hello, Little Moon Wind," and step inside the teepee.

Before my eyes can get used to the dark, I feel a wet, warm tongue licking my leg. Then I hear a puppy's whimper. It's Jumbo! He's right here! I've found him! I try to pick him up, but there's a rope 'round his little neck that's tied to something.

I look about the dark teepee. I'm beginning to see better. Little Moon Wind is curled up on a bed of some sort on the floor. Her mother is sitting on the ground beside her. It's hard to believe they're the ones who stole Jumbo away from Sammy. But it must be so, 'cause here's Jumbo in their teepee. It makes me feel sad all over.

"I came to see how Little Moon Wind is." I figure that's as good a way to start as any. "Did the sugar cubes my mama fixed help her cough?"

The mother turns her head from side to side. "No give to Little Moon Wind. Medicine man make her well when we go village."

"Oh, I'm glad he can make her well," I say, but I don't believe it for a minute. Only a regular doctor, like Doc Summers, can do that.

I reach down and pat Jumbo's head. "This dog that you ... ah ... found belongs to my friend, Sammy." I wait for her to say something, but she sits there like she's whittled out of wood. "Jumbo means a lot to Sammy," I say,

"He's the only thing Sammy's ever had of his own. Since Jumbo's been . . . ah . . . lost, Sammy's heart's been broken."

Just then, Little Moon Wind starts to cough. I never heard such a choking sound in all my life. She seems much worse than when she was at our kitchen door a few days ago. Her mother reaches inside a little pull-string bag, takes out something that looks like a piece of bark, and hands it to her. Little Moon Wind sticks it in her mouth and sucks on it between coughing fits. It's hard to believe, but it seems to help her.

"I'm sure you don't know that Sammy Stevens has a brain problem," I start again. "He's not as smart as other children his age. All he's ever had to love is Jumbo, and Jumbo loves him back."

I can't tell if the mother understands what I'm saying. But I figure it's time to try to make a trade. "I'd like to trade these beautiful ribbons and beads for Jumbo so I can take him back to my friend, Sammy." I open the cigar box. Even in the gloomy teepee the ribbons and beads glow with color. Little Moon Wind lifts up her head and takes a peek. She smiles. I have high hopes I can make a trade.

There's an old saying, "When hopes are high, don't always count on winning, 'cause it's a long ways down to losing, so you'd better stop your grinning." Actually, I made that up myself. Even so, it turns out to be true when the mother shakes her head and says, "No trade. Puppy make Little Moon Wind happy. She no can play with children. She watch puppy. She pet puppy. She keep puppy."

I can tell the visit's over. "I'd like to come and see Little Moon Wind again. Maybe tomorrow after school?" I ask. I really do want to see her. And maybe, just maybe, there's still a chance of getting Jumbo back.

The mother nods. I can come.

I start to shut the cigar box. Little Moon Wind lifts her head again like she wants to look at the ribbons and beads one more time. I feel so sorry for her that I don't think about them not being mine to give away. I take a yellow, a blue, and a red ribbon, and a string of glass beads, walk over to her bed, and lay them beside her.

"These are for you," I tell her. She puts a little hand on her treasures and closes her eyes.

As I start for the door flap, I reach down and pet Jumbo goodbye. He licks my hand and whines, like he's sorry to see me go. Then, I step outside the teepee, wipe my watery eyes, and head up the trail for the mine.

15

Jumping To Conclusions

As I hike along, I keep thinkin' 'bout coming back to the Ute camp tomorrow after school to see Little Moon Wind again. I'm happy her mother said that I could. Maybe I'll bring her some of Mama's sugar cookies. I know when I'm not feeling good, they make me feel better. Bet they'd make Little Moon Wind feel better, too. Anyway, it's worth a try.

By the time I start down the trail to the mine, the sun's getting ready to dip behind the hills. Ella and Sammy are sitting by the spring ditch. They must have got tired waiting for me inside the gloomy mine. When Sammy sees I don't have Jumbo in my arms, he lets out a screech. He jumps up, whirls and stumbles up the path toward town. I can hear him sobbing long after he's out of sight.

"What happened?" Ella whispers. "Where's Jumbo?"

I hand her the cigar box. "Little Moon Wind's mother wouldn't give him up."

Ella peeks inside the box. I can tell she's counting her ribbons and beads. She starts to say something, then shuts the lid without a word. I know I should tell her why some of her treasures are missing. But I'm afraid if I say how awful sick Little Moon Wind is, I'll start bawling.

I look into one of the quiet pools near the spring. It's like lookin' into a mirror. For the first time, I see my orange cheeks and lips. "Oh, no," I say, "everybody will laugh at me. 'Specially those bratty boys." I dip my hands in the water and try to wash the dye off. But it's soaked so deep in my skin, it won't wash off.

Ella shakes her head. "Actually, it doesn't look too bad. It gives you some much needed color." Then she does something that proves what a really true friend she is.

She's brought our dress-up clothes from the mine. She pulls another petal from the poppies on her straw, and swishes it around in the spring.

Then she rubs it over her cheeks and lips. Now her peachy skin is bright orange like mine.

"If those bratty boys say one word about our faces, they'll be sorry!" she says.

By the time we make the long trip back to town, Main Street is empty. Most folks are home either cooking supper or eating it. Ella hurries on to the funeral parlor. I duck into the restaurant. When Mama and Papa see my painted face, they're so busy with the customers, they don't stop to scold me. Leastwise, not then.

Later that night, Papa comes to tuck me in. But instead of fussing with my covers and kissing me goodnight, he sits down on the edge of my bed. This means he has something to say. Prob'ly about my orange face. So, I start talking before he can. "Papa, did you know the Utes stole Sammy's dog? His heart's broken."

"No, I hadn't heard, Gertie," he tells me. "I'm sorry. I know how much that dog means to Sammy. Maybe Mr. Stevens can get him back. The Indians had no right to take him. We try to get along with them, but we shouldn't let them get away with something like this."

I nod. "That's how I feel, Papa."

"Now," Papa says, "about your orange face …"

"Oh, it's just some orange dye I put on my face when Ella and I played dress-up in the mine this afternoon," I say.

"You'd better wash it off," he says.

I tell him, "I already tried, Papa, but it won't wash off."

"Then it'll have to wear off." He shakes his head. "I hope you've learned a lesson, Gertie."

I smile up at him. "Yes, Papa."

He stands up and starts across the room to tuck Pauline in. I know I can't let him go before I tell him about my trip to the Ute camp. A story like that is bound to get around town. Ella's prob'ly told her folks already, and Sammy might even blab it to the bratty boys. I figure if Papa hears it from me, it might go better for me.

"I felt so sorry for Sammy today," I start, "He was bawling over Jumbo. I'm 'bout the only friend he has. I wanted to do something to help him get his dog back."

"I know, sweetheart," Papa says, "but there are some things you just have to leave to the grownups. You certainly wouldn't want to do anything foolish like go to the Ute camp."

I squish my eyes shut, and duck under my covers.

Papa doesn't miss a thing. He pulls my covers off my face. "Gertie, don't tell me you went to that Ute Camp!"

"Well, Papa . . ." I start.

He points his first finger at me and shakes it hard. "Haven't I told you over and over to keep your distance from the Indians? They're different from us. We don't understand their ways, and they don't understand ours."

"But, Papa, I don't think we're so different . . ." I try to tell him.

"The fact remains," he cuts me off, "I don't want you going to their camp ever again. Especially alone. It could be dangerous. Do you understand?"

"I guess so, Papa."

He shakes his finger at me again, then heads for Pauline.

I duck back under my covers. I need to talk to God. I figure only He can fix the things that need fixin'. "Dear God, please help Little Moon Wind get well so she won't cough and choke all the time. And please help her mama do the right thing and give Jumbo back to Sammy. That little puppy is all Sammy has of his own to love. And, God, please make those bratty boys be nice to Ella and me when they see our painted faces at school tomorrow. Amen."

I didn't know it then, but what was about to happen the next day would make our painted faces the last thing on anybody's mind. Even the bratty boys' minds, such as their bratty minds are.

The next morning I climb out onto the balcony to take a peek at the day. There's a huddle of folks across the street in front of the bakery shop. Ella's father, Mr. Neil, is one of them. From the way they're all waving their arms and tossing their heads, I can tell they're upset or excited about something. Later, as I'm leaving for school, they're still there, arms waving, heads tossing. That's when somebody in the huddle shouts, "Look, there's Gertie! Hey, Gertie, come over here!"

As I cross the street, I'm thinking they'll prob'ly wonder 'bout my painted face. But not one of them seems to notice. Mr. Neil puts his arm 'round my shoulders and says, "Tell the folks, Gertie, how the Utes stole poor Sammy's dog, Jumbo, and how you went to their camp but they wouldn't give him back."

"Well," I start, but Mr. Dinwiddie cuts in, "We can't let them savages get away with this! I say we ride out to their camp and get that dog. If they try to stop us, we'll teach them a thing or two!"

A man with a rifle raises it in a most unfriendly say. "I'm ready!" he shouts.

Just then Mr. Stevens and Sammy come strolling up the sidewalk. "What's all the excitement about?" Mr. Stevens asks, smiling and waving to the crowd.

Mr. Neil hurries over to him and grabs his arm. "We heard about those Indians stealing poor Sammy's dog. Some of us are going out to their camp and get Jumbo back, whether they want to give him up or not!"

"I'm ready!" the man with the rifle shouts again.

Someone behind him yells, "Let's go!"

"Whoa!" calls Mr. Stevens. "Hold on, folks."

Everybody gets quiet.

"Those Utes didn't steal Jumbo," Mr. Stevens says. "I gave them the dog."

I never heard such gasping in all my life. I have to say, some of it came from me.

"What do you mean you gave Sammy's dog to the Utes?"

"Why on earth would you do such a thing?"

"You mean the Utes didn't steal Jumbo?"

The questions tumble and stumble over each other.

Mr. Stevens holds up his hand. "Wait a minute, folks, let me explain." He looks around at the frowning faces. "Remember someone dumping a crate of chickens in the spillway this past Halloween? Well, I just found out the other day that it was Sammy who did it."

Sammy is standing there staring down at his feet. Knowing him like I do, I'm sure he's fighting back the tears. That's when a thought strikes me like a bolt of lightning! I step out in front of the crowd and say in a loud voice, "I don't believe Sammy is to blame for drowning those poor helpless chickens."

"What do you mean, Gertie?" Mr. Stevens asks.

"Just listen and you'll see." I go over and take Sammy's hand. It feels like a leaf of wilted lettuce. "Sammy, was it your idea to dump that crate of chickens in the spillway?"

"No, Gertie," he says.

"But he told me he did it," says Mr. Stevens.

"Just wait a minute more," I tell him. I turn to Sammy again. "Then why did you do it, Sammy?"

Two tears slip down his cheeks, big tears like the first raindrops that make those big splashes on the sidewalk. "They told me to."

"They? You mean the bratty boys? They told you to dump the crate of chickens in the spillway?" I ask him.

His head bobs up and down.

"I think I know Sammy 'bout as well as anybody," I tell the folks. "He's not a bad boy. It's those bratty boys who dearly love to put him up to things—bad things like drowning those poor chickens. Sammy wouldn't think to do something like that on his own. Those bratty boys made him do it."

Mr. Stevens puts his arm around Sammy. "Oh, son, I'm sorry. I never would have given Jumbo to the Indians if I'd known." He turns to the people. "I thought Sammy should be punished for what he did. I knew he couldn't earn the money to pay for the chickens, so I did the only thing I could think of—I gave his dog to that little Ute girl, the one with the bad cough."

Well, it's over, I say to myself. The Utes didn't do anything wrong after all. No one will have to go stomping into their camp, waving a gun. I'm glad about that. But I'm sorry we'll never see Jumbo peeking out of Sammy's sweater again. Poor Jumbo. Poor Sammy. They're gonna miss each other somethin' awful.

Everybody starts to walk away. That's when a Bible verse pops into my brain. It's short and easy to remember. The kind I like best. "I can do all things through Christ which strengthened me."

And you know what? It gives me an idea!

16

Gertie Rides Again!

I'M LEARNING A LOT about helping others. Sometimes someone else steps up to do the helping. Sometimes it's left up to you. Or to me.

Since everybody else is leaving poor Sammy standing there with tears running down his face, I figure this is one of those times it's left up to me. Anyway, I'm the one who's been praying for Sammy and Jumbo. I'm the one who thought of the Bible verse 'bout Jesus helping us do the things we can't do by ourselves. So, I'm the one who steps up and shouts, "Wait!" Everybody stops and turns. I think it's the first time they notice my orange face. But not one person laughs or makes a joke.

"Well, Gertie, what is it?" one of the men asks.

I take a big breath. "I think we should still try to get Jumbo back."

Some of the folks shake their heads and walk away. I'm glad the man with the rifle is one of them. But most of the folks gather back. I feel proud to be one of them.

Since they're all looking at me, I say, "Maybe if Mr. Stevens told the Utes what happened with Sammy and the chickens, and how he punished Sammy by giving them Jumbo, and how it really wasn't Sammy's fault so he shouldn't have lost his dog, maybe the Utes will give Jumbo back."

Mr. Stevens says, "Well, it's certainly worth a try. I'll be happy to pay for Jumbo if the Utes will sell him back to me."

Everybody cheers!

Just then Doc Summers pulls up in his horse and buggy. "What's all the commotion about?" he asks.

Mr. Neil tells him, "We're talking about going out to the Ute camp to try and get Sammy's dog back."

Doc Summers shakes his head. "'Fraid you'll be wasting your time. Those Utes should be miles away by now."

Everybody groans. "You mean they left?" somebody asks.

Doc Summers takes off his hat and wipes his forehead. "Think so. At least they were packing up last evening when I passed by their camp on my way to deliver Mrs. Teeter's new baby son."

Mr. Stevens asks, "Were the Utes gone when you came by on your way home after delivering the baby, Doc?"

"Came home a different way, by the Browns' farm, to check on Ernest's broken arm," he answers.

"I think someone should go to the Ute camp to see if they really left," a voice behind me says. I turn 'round. There stands Papa. His next words show what a truly kind and loving man he is. "I think Mr. Stevens, and Sammy, and Gertie should go to the camp, and I'll be happy to go with them." My Papa, who told me never to go near the Indian camp again, says we should go to that very camp and try to get Jumbo back! And he's even willing—no, even "happy"—to go with us! It's all we need to hear.

The four of us take off up Main Street with the rest of the folks yelling after us, "Good luck!"

"Bring Jumbo back!"

"God bless you!"

"Hope you make it in time!"

But will we make it in time? It's a good mile and a half to the Ute camp over a rough, hilly trail. I have a sinking feeling we'll be too late.

Just then my friend, Mr. Hansen, comes trotting up the street on his little mare, Jennie. I jump up and down, and wave my arms for him to stop.

"Can I borrow Jennie?" I ask him. "It's a matter of life or death!"

Mr. Hansen looks at Sammy's wet face, and at all the folks gathered nearby. Without a word, he slips off Jennie's back and hands me the reins. (He's used to me borrowing his little mare. He knows I'll take good care of her.)

"Now, wait a minute, Gertie," Papa lays a heavy hand on my shoulder.

"Papa, you've just got to let me go," I tell him. "If we walk there, it'll take a long time. We could be too late."

Papa bends down 'til his eyes are staring straight into mine. "Only if you promise not to try to get Jumbo back yourself. Just ask the Utes to wait. Tell them Mr. Stevens, the man who gave them the dog, is coming. Remember, don't try to get Jumbo back yourself. Gertie, do you promise?"

I pump my head up and down. "Yes, Papa, I promise."

While me and Papa are talking, Mr. Hansen shortens the stirrups to fit me. Jennie's ready and waiting. Papa helps me climb into the saddle. I bounce my heels against Jennie's sides—not too hard, just hard enough to get her movin'. And off we go!

We race up Main Street past the spillway where all the trouble started with Sammy drowning the chickens. Then on past the Baptist Church where the Thanksgiving program will be in full swing in a couple of weeks. Then out into the countryside with little dust clouds following after us.

It seems like forever 'fore I see the spring ditch ahead. As we pass the pools of clear water, millions of minnows dart this way and that way, scared by Jennie's pounding hoofs. Then up, up over the hill we fly like a soaring eagle, and down, down the rocky trail into the Ute camp.

"Whoa!" I call, and Jennie slides to a stop, snorting and puffing.

I look around. There're no women grinding acorns, no children playing, no bony horses, no tired old dog, no raggedy teepees, no smoky campfire. Only a heap of cold ashes.

"Go, Jennie!" I yell in her ear. She races through the camp and up the trail on the other side. Maybe they haven't gone too far, I figure. Maybe we can still catch them, Jennie and me.

At the top of the next hill, I rein Jennie in again. There's the Teeter farm far below. Beyond is a valley sparse of trees. I can see the trail for miles ahead. There's not one Indian on it.

Somehow I know I'll never see Little Moon Wind again. I wanted to be her friend. I think she wanted that, too. But now she's gone. And Jumbo with her.

"Goodbye, Little Moon Wind," I whisper. "Goodbye, Jumbo."

I turn Jennie around and we trot back to the empty camp. I wonder what made the Utes leave so quick. I think about how sick Little Moon Wind was the day before. I can almost see her tiny, peaked face. I can almost hear Jumbo's pitiful whine. Actually, I can hear Jumbo, only he isn't whining. He's barking!

I whirl Jennie around. There's Jumbo tied to a stake near a tree! I must have passed by him when I first rode into camp. But the noise of Jennie's hoofs and her snorting must have drowned out any sound he made. Or maybe, like the minnows, he was scared of Jennie, but instead of darting this way and that way, he huddled next to the tree, quiet and still. Well, he's not quiet and still now. He's one noisy, bouncing puppy!

I jump down off Jennie's back and throw my arms around him. He licks my face so hard, I'm sure that stubborn dye will come off at last. Poor little feller. No tellin' how long he's been tied to that stake. I untie the rope from around his neck.

That's when I see something hanging from the lower limb of the tree. But my eyes are so watery, I can't tell what it is. I wipe my eyes. It's the yellow and blue ribbons and the string of beads I gave to Little Moon Wind! The red ribbon's missing. I look 'round on the ground. It's gone. Most likely blown away by the morning breeze. I pick the ribbons and beads off the limb, and stick them in my pocket.

Little Moon Wind's mother knew I was coming to visit again today. She must have left the ribbons and beads for me to find. But why? Why didn't Little Moon Wind take them with her? I know she loves them. And why did they leave Jumbo? What does it all mean?

Jumbo's barking and jumping 'round so happy, I can't think. I pick him up and carry him while I walk Jennie over to a big rock. It takes a bit of doing, but with Jumbo slung over my shoulder, and the reins held in my teeth, I climb to the top of the rock. Then I coax Jennie in close, slip my leg over the saddle, and with the help of the saddle horn, pull myself onto Jennie's back. Then the three of us head up the trail for home.

As we trot along, I think of that picture in our Sunday School class, the one of Jesus carrying the little lost lamb in His arms.

I dearly love that picture.

17

Remembering Little Moon Wind

Have you ever wondered how you'd feel if Christmas, the circus, and your birthday came on the same day? That's how Sammy must have felt when he saw me, Jumbo, and Jennie riding up the trail. He was smiling from ear to ear. Course he was bawling, too. Actually, he wasn't the only one.

By the time we get back to town, it's almost noon.

"You might as well stay home from school the rest of the day, Gertie," Papa tells me. "I know you must be awfully tired. And maybe you can get that dye off your face."

That suits me fine. But first I have to take Jennie back to Mr. Hansen. I know he'll be happy to hear how his little mare helped bring Jumbo and Sammy together again.

"My, my," he says as I tell him how me and Jennie rode through the empty Ute camp, up the trail beyond, then back to the camp where I found Jumbo tied to the stake. He pats me on the head. "You're quite a hero, Gertie."

When it's time for school to let out, I watch for Ella from the restaurant balcony. She and the Teeter twins soon come skipping up the sidewalk. Ella looks happy. I figure the bratty boys weren't too ornery about her orange cheeks and lips.

She sees me and waves. "Hi, Gertie! Wait 'til you hear what happened in class."

Leave it to Ella. I'm the one who rode all over the country chasing Indians and saving Jumbo, and she says, "Wait 'til you hear what happened in class."

But as it turns out, what happened in class is worth hearing about. Seems after I took Jennie back to Mr. Hansen, he and Jennie came trotting by the school yard. The children were still at noon recess. Miss Goldbranson was standing near the fence. Mr. Hansen called to her, "Guess you're pretty proud of Gertie." And Miss Goldbranson called back, "Proud of Gertie? Whatever for?" That's when he told her the whole Jumbo story from Sammy and the drowned chickens to my two trips to the Ute camp.

"After recess," Ella goes on, "Miss Goldbranson told us all about it. But she didn't mention my part in it," Ella rolls her eyes and shakes her head, "So I raised my hand and told her how I was with you in the mine when you put on your war paint, and how I put on some, too, in case there was trouble at the Ute camp and you needed me to help." Course Ella forgot that she put on her war paint after I came back from the Ute camp. "Oh, Gertie," she says, "you should have heard how everybody clapped. Even the bratty boys think we did something big."

The next morning it's plain to see how "big" the bratty boys think it is. They come to school with their faces painted black and white with something that looks and smells like shoe polish.

I'm sure Miss Goldbranson will have a fit. But she doesn't. She says, "Class, because of your apparent interest in the Ute Indians, we are going to study their history and culture. I'm hoping that Gertie will start us off by telling about her visits to the Ute camp."

My face is hot as fire.

I don't like to get up in front of the class. But I figure I might as well do what Miss Goldbranson wants. She's gonna have her way no matter what.

As I tell my story, I keep sharing more and more about Little Moon Wind. How sick she is. How poor her family is. How she smiled so pitiful when I gave her the ribbons and beads. That's when Ella sticks her arm up, wiggles her fingers, and says where the ribbons and beads came from. And that's when I say that when I found Jumbo, I found the ribbons and beads hanging from a tree.

"But if she liked them so much," says Tilly or Lilly Teeter (I can't tell them apart when they got the same clothes on), "why didn't she take them with her?"

Since I'm wondering, too, I just lift up my shoulders and scrunch up my face.

That's when Miss Goldbranson says something that makes me feel sick all over. "Doc Summers believes the little Ute girl died. That's why they broke camp so suddenly. That's why they left Jumbo and the ribbons and beads behind."

I can't say another word. I put my head down and make a beeline for my desk. Ella reaches out and pats my hand, but it doesn't help. I have an awful hurt in my heart I know will never go away. It's that awful hurt that makes me want to talk to Grandma Larson so bad that I hike out to her house as soon as school is over.

"Gertie, what a nice surprise," Grandma says when she finds me at her front door. "You're just in time for some sugar cookies, fresh and warm from the oven."

"Grandma, I don't want any cookies," I tell her, "I came because I need to ask you something important."

"Well, come on in, sweetheart." She opens the door and I step inside. "Sit here on the sofa," she pats a spot beside her. "Now, what is it you want to ask me?"

I take a deep breath. "What about death?"

"Ahhh," she says like she knows I was gonna ask that very thing. "Death, yes, it needs to be looked at from time to time. And now is one of those times? Is that what you're telling me?"

"Uh huh," I answer.

She puts her arms around me and gives me a hug. "Death may seem strange and mysterious to us, Gertie, but it's just a natural part of life. Think of it as an unknown adventure waiting around the corner. We don't know exactly what's there, but from what we learn in the Bible, it's nothing to fear." She gives me another hug. "When we who love God die, our spirit goes to heaven to live with Him forever. So, in many ways, death is not an ending but a beginning—a beginning of a happier and more beautiful life than we've ever known or could imagine."

"What about Indians?" I ask.

She says, "Do you mean, do they go to heaven?"

"Uh huh," I answer.

"Well," she says, "God loves Indians just like He loves all the peoples of the world. And like all the peoples of the world, those who trust Jesus to be their Savior are bound for heaven!"

"What about little children?" I ask.

"Oh, yes, little children go to heaven," she tells me. "Remember what Jesus said, 'Suffer little children, and forbid them not, to come unto Me, for of such is the Kingdom of heaven.' Little children most certainly go to heaven."

I'm starting to feel some better. But I still have one more question to ask, "Grandma, if death is so wonderful, why do we feel so sad when somebody dies?"

"Ahhh," she says, "that's because we're feeling sorry for ourselves. Sorry that we'll never see that loved one again. At least not in this old world." She throws me a sweet grandma smile. "Well, Gertie, does that help you understand death better?"

"I guess so," I tell her. "But, Grandma, that's a lot of hard stuff for me to get into my brain. I'm not as smart as you. I'm not even as smart as Ella. She gets 'A's' in school all the time. I'm doing good if I ever get a 'B.'"

"Well, Gertie," Grandma says, "always remember, there are two kinds of smart—head smart and heart smart. Ella may have lots of head smart. But you have lots of heart smart. And that's just as good." She gives me a kiss on the cheek. "I've watched how you treat Sammy with kindness no matter what he says or does. And how you befriended Little Moon Wind when she was so sick. And how patient you are with Ella who, heaven knows, is not the easiest person to be around. Yes, Gertie, you've been blessed with an extra portion of heart smart. And I praise and thank the Lord for it!"

On my way home, I think of how Grandma's many years of living have added up to a lot of understanding—both in her head and in her heart, too. And I praise and thank the Lord for it!

18

The Thanksgiving Program

THE NEXT FEW DAYS I keep thinking 'bout Little Moon Wind, and what Grandma Larson said about death and heaven. Grandma's words did make me feel better. But they didn't make me feel good—not about Little Moon Wind dying.

There is one thing I do feel good about though. I finished my "What I Have To Be Thankful For" essay, and gave it to Miss Goldbranson.

"Well, Gertie, I'm very proud of you, although your essay does seem a bit short."

There are people in this world who always add words like "although" or "however" or "but" when they tell you something nice. Miss Goldbranson is one.

Now that I finished my essay, the Thanksgiving program doesn't seem like such a bad idea. In fact, I wish it would hurry and get here. I still feel awful about Little Moon Wind. I'm hoping the program, 'specially the pie sociable, will help me feel better.

At last it's the day before Thanksgiving. Store windows are spruced-up with autumn leaves, house porches are prettied-up with stalks of Indian corn, and on church steps and along fences and sidewalks, pumpkins are lined-up, orange and shiny. Best of all, ladies are busy popping pies in and out of ovens all over town.

Mama bakes four pumpkin pies. Two to take to the pie sociable. Two to keep. Not for the customers. For us!

That evening Papa says, "It's time to go." He puts the *"Closed"* sign in the front restaurant window. Mama sets her pies, along with Lorraine, in the baby buggy. "Now, don't stick your fingers or toes in my pies," she tells the baby. We all laugh.

When we get to the Fellowship Hall, it's already filling up with people. Folks are waving and calling to each other across the big room, "Great night for the program!"

"Can hardly wait to sink my teeth into one of those pies!"

I look around for Ella. Instead I see something that surprises, then puzzles, then makes me very happy. Who should be sitting three rows back, all dolled up in a striped shirt with his hair slicked down, but Sammy Stevens. That surprises me. Sammy never comes inside to programs and such. He always stays on the outside peekin' in. And he's holding one of Widow Gustafson's little children on his lap. That puzzles me. Sammy never gets that close to anybody. 'Cept Jumbo, of course. Just then, Widow Gustafson, reaches over and pats Sammy on his cheek. That tender pat brings a look to his face I can never ever put into words. But it makes me very happy just the same.

Miss Goldbranson is standing at the front of the hall with her hand up for folks to be quiet. "Doc Summers has a special announcement," she says. The minute they hear Doc Summers' name, everybody settles down. It's that prestige thing again.

"Friends," Doc starts, "you've all been interested in how our little heroine, Gertie Larson, helped to get Sammy Steven's beloved dog, Jumbo, back from the Utes. There was only one thing that kept this from being a truly happy story—the apparent death of Little Moon Wind, the sick Ute child."

Somebody sobs. It's me. I just can't hold it in. Hearing 'bout Little Moon Wind's death in a "special announcement" makes it hurt all the more.

"Wait a minute, Gertie," Doc calls to me, "you haven't heard the good news. Little Moon Wind is alive!"

Folks "ooh" and "ahh" all over the hall. Ella comes running from somewhere on the other side of the room. She throws her arms around me, lays her head on my shoulder, and cries. Little trickles of her happy tears run down my cheek. Along with some of my own.

"A couple of days ago I went to Salt Lake City on business," Doc is saying. "About ten miles north of town, I was looking out the train window when I noticed several teepees up ahead. Two little Indian children were standing near the tracks waving at the train going by. Ordinarily I would have just glanced at them. But something caught my eye and caused me to look more closely. That's when I recognized Little Moon Wind."

Me and Ella hug and cry some more.

"Yes, I believe it was an act of Providence that I noticed her," Doc says. "Providence and that bright red ribbon she was wearing right on the top of her head where you couldn't miss it."

Ella jumps up and down and waves her hands. I figure she's gonna say it was her ribbon. But instead she yells, "Gertie gave her that ribbon!" Everybody cheers. I feel like I could fly if I could flap my arms fast and hard enough.

So that's what happened to the red ribbon, I say to myself. It didn't blow away. Little Moon Wind took it with her. Maybe to remember me by. And maybe her mother left Jumbo 'cause she felt sorry for Sammy after I told her 'bout his hurt brain and broken heart. Yes, sir, it was an act of kindness. An Indian act of kindness. I was right. Indians aren't so different from us after all.

The program lasts well over an hour. Penny Peterson reads a poem about her dead cat, Sybil. It's supposed to be sad, but I hear some giggling. Prob'ly the bratty boys. Mr. Langston, the blacksmith, plays two songs on his flute. Mrs. Lomeli's first grade class sings a song in Spanish, "El Provo," which means "The Turkey." Pauline is in Mrs. Lomeli's class. Pauline gets to do the solo—the "gobble gobble" part—which sounds about the same in Spanish as it does in English. We're very proud of Pauline. There are other fine acts—the Teeter twins' piano duet, a square dance demonstration by the Richfield Rompers, and some slight of hand tricks by Mr. Cavnar, the butcher. (That's when Aunt Danny whispers so loud everybody close by can hear her, "*That butcher's hands are so quick and nimble makes me wonder how really free the soup bones are he's always bragging about.*" Then she laughs and I know she's only fooling.)

Near the end of the program, Editor Richards talks about the fine essays the fifth grade children wrote, and what a hard time he had picking the winner and the four runners-up. Then he asks Ella to come and read her winning essay. Yes, Ella's the winner of the "What I Have To Be Thankful For" essay contest. Which doesn't surprise me.

Ella prances up the stairs and onto the stage, curls bouncing, skirt flouncing. She curtsies, and begins to read, page after page after page. Every so often, she livens things up by whirling around, or marching in place, or falling on the floor like in a dead faint. (Miss Goldbranson told us later these are called "dramatic gestures.")

It takes Ella so long to read her essay and the pies smell so good, Editor Richards says he's sorry, but it's getting too late to have the four runners-up read their essays. I'm glad, because I'm one of the four runners-up.

Well, it turns out to be a wonderful Thanksgiving program. And the best is yet to come. The pie sociable! Tables are loaded with slices of every kind of pie. I grab a chair and slide it next to Mary's.

"I'm sorry you didn't win the essay contest, Gertie," she tells me. She takes a big bite of a slice of Mama's pumpkin pie. I do the same.

Ella's still standing in the middle of the stage. Folks are gathered 'round her, shaking her hand and hugging her. As my Aunt Danny would say, "She's in her glory." Which means she's lapping it up.

Mary sees me watching Ella. She gives me a hope-this-will-comfort-you pat on my back. I figure she figures I feel bad about not winning the essay contest and the five dollar cash prize. Actually, I don't feel bad. I feel happy. Hearing that Little Moon Wind is alive and well is all the prize I could ever want in the whole wide world.

19

It Gets Even Better

WHEN *THE RICHFIELD REAPER* comes out the following Monday, there's Ella's essay on the front page. Actually, it's only part of it. "Due to its abundant length," it says in the newspaper, "the remainder of the winning essay will appear in serial form over the next several weeks." I'm very proud of Ella. So is she.

That night after the restaurant closes, me, Mama, Papa, Aunt Danny, Grandma and Grandpa Larson, Mary, and Pauline sit 'round the kitchen table. Lorraine's in bed asleep. Aunt Danny starts talking about the Thanksgiving program.

"Ella's essay was nice," she says, "a bit long, but nice."

"What pie did you like best?" Mama asks.

We all agree it was her pumpkin.

While we talk about the piano duet, and the slight of hand tricks, and the poem Penny wrote about her cat, Papa glances through the newspaper. All at once he says, "Well, I'll be!"

"What is it, Lars?" Mama wants to know. She's still smiling from the winning vote on her pumpkin pie.

Papa looks 'round the table. "I want all of you to listen to this," he tells us. "It's the Thanksgiving essay of one of the four runners-up. It's printed here on the back page." He clears his throat and starts to read, "The things I have to be thankful for can't be seen or touched or worn. They are things here inside me like memories and dreams and lessons I've learned."

Papa's reading my essay!

"The memories are of my family and friends and the times we shared. No matter where I go or what I do, these memories will keep me company for the rest of my life." Papa takes out his handkerchief and blows his nose. Then he reads on, "One of my dreams is to be a circus star when I grow up and do tricks on the trapeze."

"It's Gertie!" Mary says.

Everybody turns and looks at me. Aunt Danny reaches in her purse, takes out a penny, and sets it on the table in front of me.

"Well, go on, Lars," Mama says. I can tell she's taking this big. Her shoulders aren't as droopy from standing over the stove all day as they mostly are this time of night.

"I have other dreams, too," Papa starts reading again, "like some day I want to be a mother like Mama. Mama works hard with Papa in the restaurant. She takes good care of our family. I can always go to her when I need something, if she's not too busy at the stove cooking for the customers. As tired as she gets, she never complains. I am proud to say, my Mama has prestige."

There's more nose blowing, this time all 'round the table. Three more pennies join the first one.

Papa goes on reading, "The lessons I've learned, not school lessons but lessons of life, I learned mostly from my family—Papa, Mama, my sisters, Grandma and Grandpa Larson, and Aunt Danny—about love and patience and kindness and forgiveness. And that life is full of adventures waiting around the corner. And that even death is an adventure we don't have to fear if we have faith in the Lord Jesus Who overcame death on the cross that we might have life with Him forever in heaven."

Right then, a wonderful thing happens. Everybody reaches out and holds hands. Nobody says to do it. We just do it.

Then Papa reads on, "I learned from Ella Neil that a real true friend will paint her face orange so you won't be made fun of alone. Little Moon Wind taught me that we may be different on the outside, but inside we have the same feelings. It's like we're cut from the same pattern, but from different cloth. Sammy Stevens taught me that life is like a bowl of ice cream. It might not be the flavor you want, and your bowl might not be as full as the bowls of folks smarter or better off than you, but it's your bowl. So, bow your head and give thanks to the good Lord for what you have. Then pick up your spoon and dive in!"

At first nobody says anything. Then Mary whispers, "Dear Jesus, thank You for my family." And Mama says, "Lord, forgive me for worrying that You won't provide all that we need." Then Aunt Danny says, "Thank You, Lord, for the promise of eternal life," and Grandpa and Grandma Larson add an "Amen." I think it's 'cause they're old and figure they're most likely the next leaves to fall from the family tree.

There's more praying 'round the table, but I can't remember it all, 'cept what Papa says at the end. "Thank You, Lord, for Gertie. She's taught us all a good lesson."

The next morning I wake up with a heart full of joyful thanksgiving! I think about Jumbo peeking out of Sammy's sweater again. About Little Moon Wind watching the train go by, wearing my red ribbon. About the pennies—seven in all!—that Aunt Danny stacked on the table in front of me as Papa read my essay in *The Richfield Reaper*.

I climb out my window onto the balcony. It's another sun-shiny day. I look up and down Main Street. Here comes Sammy plodding along the sidewalk. He stops in front of the saloon. Oh, no, he's peeking under the swinging doors again. I wait for someone inside to yell, "Get away from here, crazy!" But instead, one of the waiters comes out. He says something to Sammy, and Sammy nods and pulls his sweater open. Out pokes Jumbo. The waiter laughs and scratches Jumbo on the head. Then he hauls something out of his trouser pocket and hands it to Sammy. They wave goodbye, and Sammy hurries up the street and into the ice cream parlor.

As long as I can remember, I never saw anybody treat Sammy like this before. Like a friend. 'Cept me, of course. And Widow Gustafson. True, when folks saw him riding with me in the circus parade on my birthday, they cheered and waved at him. But not as a friend, exactly. Maybe now when they heard some of us were ready to take on the Utes to get his dog back, and saw him at the Thanksgiving program all slicked up, and read about him in my Thanksgiving essay in the newspaper, they figure he's as much God's child as anybody else, hurt brain and all. Leastwise, they're treating him kinder. And he's happier for it. I haven't seen him bawl in weeks.

Hearing that waiter's friendly laugh makes me think people are happier, too. Maybe God gives us a greater blessing when we give a kindness than when we get one. Like that saying, "It's more blessed to give than to receive." That may even be in the Bible. But I'm not sure. But I bet it is. Leastwise, it could be.

Well, if you haven't figured it out yet, that's how my second real life adventure ends—with lots of good things happening, and me smack dab in the middle of 'em.

Now, I'm off on my third real life adventure! Are you comin'?

20

Who, Me?

REMEMBER HOW I SAID real life adventures can come in a bunch? Well, along with my first and second adventures, my third adventure was part of the bunch, too.

It happened 'bout eight months after I galloped into the Ute camp to get Sammy's dog, Jumbo, back. Now, you may think that eight months between real life adventures is too long a time to count 'em as a bunch. But remember, there's always some little adventures that help the big ones along. So, you gotta count them, too. And when you count the little ones with the big ones, they sorta bunch together. See?

Anyway, my third big real life adventure starts with Sammy's papa stopping by our restaurant for a cup of coffee. I'm busy clearing the dirty dishes off the tables. The supper crowd's mostly gone. Papa sits down for a minute to visit with Mr. Stevens. That's when I hear Mr. Stevens say something that makes my eyes pop open.

"You know, Lars," he says, "I've been thinking about having a birthday party for Sammy. He'll be fourteen in about a month. August 17th to be exact. He's never had a party before. I never gave him one because, frankly, I never thought any of the children would want to come. I wasn't sure Sammy'd even want one." He throws Papa what I call a wobbly smile—one that can't make up its mind if it's happy or sad.

I want to step up and tell him that everybody wants a birthday party. Everybody. Even somebody like Sammy, hurt brain and all. But it's not polite to butt in when grownups are talking. Leastwise, not unless they ask you to.

Just then Mary sticks a tray under my nose. "Are you ever gonna help me fill this tray so I can haul the dirty dishes into the kitchen and wash and dry them?" She sounds cross. I know she's tired.

By the time we get the dishes stacked on the tray, Mr. Stevens has gulped the last of his coffee, scraped back his chair, grabbed his hat, and is out the door strolling up Main Street. I can hardly wait to ask Papa what he said 'bout a birthday party for Sammy. But a late supper rush keeps us so busy, it isn't 'til Papa comes to tuck me in bed that night that I have a chance to ask him.

"Papa, is Mr. Stevens really gonna give Sammy a birthday party?"

Papa bends his tall, thin body over my bed. He lays his hand on my head, brushes my hair out of the way, and plants a goodnight kiss on my forehead. "He's thinking about it."

"Well, when's he gonna make up his mind?" I ask.

Papa says, "Believe it or not, Gertie, that depends on you."

"What do you mean, Papa?" I ask. "How does it depend on me?"

"Mr. Stevens says you're about the best friend Sammy ever had," Papa starts. "Sammy thinks the world of you. He seems able to talk to you better than to his own papa. So, Mr. Stevens asked me to ask you to find out what Sammy thinks about having a birthday party, especially if he'd even like one, who he'd want to invite, and what kind of party he'd like. You know, what games and such."

"But, Papa," I say, "can't a grownup, like Widow Gustafson, talk to Sammy 'bout all that? Sammy likes her a lot. She's awful tender toward him, too, almost like the mama he never knew. I'm just a little girl. I can't . . ."

Papa jumps in, "I know it's a big order, Gertie. But if anyone can do it, you can. Just ask Sammy a few questions without actually saying he's going to have a party. His papa doesn't want to plan something Sammy won't be happy with. Well, what do you say? Can I tell Mr. Stevens you'll help him?" He throws me a sweet papa smile.

There are times when you just can't argue with your papa or your mama. And it's plain this is one of those times. So, I tell Papa, "I guess so."

When Papa's gone, I slip out of bed onto my knees. If I'm gonna help, I gotta get some help first. I look out my window. The night sky is sprinkled with tiny bits of light, dozens of 'em. Here I am, just a speck of a little girl on a speck of a little world, floating in acres and acres of space. Even so, God promises to listen when I talk to Him. So that's what I do. "Dear God, my friend Sammy's never had a birthday party in all his life. His papa wants to give him one. He's not sure what kind of a party Sammy'd like, or even if he'd want one. He wants me to find out. I don't know how. Please help me. Amen."

That's when Ella's name pops into my head, which doesn't surprise me. Ella, to hear her tell it, plans the biggest and best birthday parties in all of Richfield. I have to say, she does have a way of making a birthday party special. But I need to know for sure if it's God Who put her name in my brain. I figure the best way to find out is to tell Ella 'bout Mr. Steven's birthday idea, and see what she says. So, that's what I do on our way to Sunday School the next morning.

"Mr. Stevens must be crazy!" is the first thing she says. "A birthday party for Sammy? Who will do the decorations, make out the guest list, choose the kind of party that'll fit Sammy best—if there even is one—and most important, plan the birthday activity? You don't just have a party, especially for somebody like Sammy. You have to plan, organize, figure things out."

Now I know for sure it was God Who put her name in my brain. Nobody figures out birthday party plans like Ella. Though she sounds like the idea's a bad one, her blinking eyes and bouncing curls tell me she's excited 'bout it. I know when she hears I'm sorta in charge, she'll want to help. But I know, too, if I act like I need her to help, she'll think she can boss the whole thing. So, I start talking about something else.

"Are you and your folks going to the community dance Saturday night?" I ask.

Her eyes stop blinking and stare at me big and round. "Huh?"

So, I ask her again.

"Oh, I suppose so," she answers. "Did you say when Sammy's birthday is?"

I shrug. "No, I don't think I did."

"Well?" She stops walking, kicks out one foot, and starts tapping it on the sidewalk. "When is it?"

"August 17th," I tell her.

"Hmmm, that gives Mr. Stevens a little over a month to plan," she says.

I figure I best tell her now. "Actually, he wants me to sorta take charge of things; find out from Sammy if he'd even want a party, and if he does, what kind he'd like."

Ella squeezes her mouth into a little circle. "Well, of course, you are Sammy's best friend. I suppose that's why Mr. Stevens asked you to help instead of a more experienced party planner." Then off to church she skips, with me running to catch up.

For the rest of the morning, Ella acts like she's forgotten all about Sammy's birthday party. But I know Ella. She can't let party plans be made without her hand in them. Sure enough, later on our way home she says, "I guess I could help you."

I know if I'm gonna be in charge, I can't let her waltz in and take over. I gotta slow her down. And I know just how to do it. "But, Ella," I tell her, "you've said over and over that Sammy makes you feel 'uncomfortable.' I didn't think you'd want to help."

She blows out a big sigh. Her eyes are watery. "Everybody should have at least one birthday party before he dies. Being born is a big event. Even for Sammy. He's never had a birthday party. It's time he had one. And if you want me to, I'll help."

I feel awful. I thought Ella wanted to help only because she likes parties. Anybody's party. Even Sammy's. But I can tell from her watery eyes, Ella feels sorry for Sammy.

"If Mr. Stevens makes up his mind to have a birthday party for Sammy," I tell her, "I know he'll be happy to have both of us helping. And with both of us helping, it'll be the best birthday party ever!"

Ella's face turns from cloudy-frowny to sunny-smiley. I feel better, too.

21

The Community Dance

IT'S A FUNNY THING. When you don't want to see somebody, you run into him every time you turn around. When you do want to see somebody, you never run into him no matter how many times you turn around. That's the way it was with me and Sammy. All that week I look for him. All that week I don't see him once. In a way I'm glad. I really don't want to talk to him even though I promised I would. You know, to find out if he wants a birthday party or not, and if so, what kind.

Then it's Saturday night. Time for the community dance. This month it's at the Snows'. They've cleared their large living and dining rooms of the furniture so the thirty or so folks who most often come can two-step and waltz without getting their feet all tangled. At first I spend time with the other children, sitting on the floor, with our legs tucked under us, leaning against the wall, watchin' the dancers stomp and glide by. Then I head for the kitchen. There's a table there loaded with pies and cakes the ladies have brought. I'm just finishing a piece of vanilla cake when I see Sammy peeking in the kitchen window. This might be a good time to find out how he feels about having a birthday party.

I wave for him to meet me on the back porch. Then I head out the kitchen door. We sit, side by side, on the steps goin' down into the back yard. I figure I'll start right off by asking him what he thinks about birthday parties.

"Well, Sammy," I say, "what do you think about birthday parties?"

He lifts his shoulders up, then drops them. "I don't think about 'em, Gertie."

"Well, what I mean is, do you like them?" I ask.

He blinks his eyes like he's thinking hard. "I liked yours, Gertie."

"Well, yes, but mine was extra special. You don't ride an elephant in a circus parade every birthday," I tell him. "I guess my birthday party was the only one you've ever been to. But you've seen other children having birthday parties, haven't you? Like at the ice cream parlor or at the spring ditch or in their back yards?"

"Yes, Gertie," he says.

"Well, then," I ask, "what kind of a party do you like best?"

"I like yours best, Gertie," he tells me again.

I say, "I mean besides mine, like a picnic in the meadow or a hike to the abandoned mine or a cookout at Eagle Tree."

He slides his fingers into his hair and scratches back and forth. At last he says, "I like yours best, Gertie."

Oh, for heaven's sake, I think. How am I ever gonna get him off the circus parade and onto some idea his papa can handle? I take his hand and lead him into the kitchen. That's when he says something that makes my heart ache.

"I never had a birthday party, Gertie. If I ever do, I want one like yours, with a parade."

Well, I give up. I slice him a piece of strawberry cake, grab him a fork, give him a push out the kitchen door, and send him on his way.

I'm finishing off a hunk of apple pie, when Ella comes through the door.

"Well," I tell her, "I talked to Sammy about birthday parties."

"What did he say? Does he want one? Did he tell you what kind he'd like? Did he say where he'd like to have it?"

As soon as she stops to gulp some air, I jump in. "Oh, he'd like a party all right, if he can have one like mine!"

She grabs at her throat. "You don't mean with a circus parade!"

"Well, with a parade, anyway," I say. "It's the only kind of party he wants."

"Then that's that," she says, swinging her curly head from side to side. "Guess poor Sammy will never ever have a birthday party."

I nod. "Guess not."

"When are you gonna tell Sammy's papa?" she asks. She's piled two slices of chocolate cake on a plate and is aiming her fork for a bite.

"Soon as I get a chance to," I tell her.

All at once, the music for the dancing stops. We hear talking coming from the living room. Mr. Snow is asking for volunteers to hold the next dance, and for musicians to play for the dancing. It doesn't take long for Doc Summers to say they can have it at his house, and for Mrs. Summers to say she'll play the piano. It makes me think of how kind and generous Richfield folks are. They're always ready to take a turn, give a helping hand, open their homes, or bake a pie or cake.

Later, on the way home, I tell Papa about my talk with Sammy.

"I was afraid it wouldn't be easy," Papa says. "Do you think you could talk Sammy into some other kind of party? One without a parade?"

"I don't know, Papa," I tell him. "He seems pretty set in his ways. Like it's a birthday party same as mine, or nothing."

Papa rolls his eyes, like he's thinkin' hard. "Well, Gertie," he says at last, "I know Mr. Stevens will be grateful for all you tried to do. You'll just have to tell him that Sammy wants a birthday party only if it comes with a parade."

I go to bed that night hoping and praying there's some way to give Sammy the birthday party he wants. I figure there must be a way to do it. I just need to figure out what that way is.

The next morning I wake up with an idea rumbling 'round inside my brain. At first I try to shove it away, but it won't shove. Not that it isn't a good idea. It's just that it's a big idea that'll take a lot of doing to do. I'm just a little girl. I was hoping for a little idea that'll take a little bit of doing to do.

It's the folks at the community dance who gave me the idea; how they're willing to work together to put on the dance. If I can get enough folks to work together that way, maybe, just maybe, Sammy can have the birthday party he wants.

I figure not to say anything to anybody about my idea 'til I talk to Ella. She's quick to pick things apart. If my idea isn't any good, she'll be first to say so.

On our way to Sunday School, I tell her all about it. "Hmmm," she says, "a community birthday parade. It just might work."

I grin so hard my cheeks cramp. If Ella thinks it might work, it really might! All we have to do is get the community behind it. Or as Ella puts it, "Find enough folks willing to march in a parade for a boy who has a hurt brain, who hardly talks, who bawls a lot, and who drowned a crate of chickens in the spillway last Halloween." Then she says something that shows what a smart thinker she is. "Maybe we can get the store owners along Main Street to join in if they think it'll help their business. You know, make them look more like caring neighbors than folks just out to make a living off the community."

"Well, it's worth a try," I tell her, "but I don't think we should say anything to Mr. Stevens 'til we see if there's enough store owners, and other folks, willing to make up a parade. I can ask my friend, Miss Ida Mae Clark, what she thinks about it. Her millinery shop's on Main Street. She's very popular with the other store owners. Whenever anybody needs a fancy bonnet, she's always willing to whip one up at the drop of a hat. She's smart, too. She can talk to folks; find out what they think about a community parade without actually telling them who it's for or why."

"I'll leave that up to you, Gertie," Ella says. "You're the one who runs errands for Miss Clark. I only know her as the millinery shop owner who gave you three or four hats for helping her, and all are raising little dust kittens under your bed."

"Well," I say, "I hate hats. I only wear one when Mama makes me."

Ella taps her forehead. "But it might be smart to wear one when you go to see Miss Clark."

Sure enough, Monday after school when Ida Mae Clark sees me standing in her doorway with her straw hat with purple lilacs perched on my head, she throws her arms around me and hugs me for all she's worth. She's not a big woman. Actually, she's very slender and on the short side. But all that sewing and stitching must be good for building arm muscles. I have to wiggle free to keep breathing.

"Gertie, dear," she says, "it's so good to see you! It's been a long while." She puts a soft palm against my cheek, then squeezes it with her strong fingers. I'm about to yell "Ouch!" when she lets go with a three-slap pat on my already smarting face. (Some folks think they have to pinch, pat, or squeeze you to show they like you.)

I figure I better get to why I'm here before she pinches my nose and makes my eyes water. Which she's done before. "Miss Clark," I say, "I have a question to ask you. Actually, a favor."

She smiles. "Well, what is it, Gertie? How can I help you? It's usually the other way around, you helping me."

"I'm studying the idea of a birthday party for Sammy Stevens," I tell her. "He'll be fourteen in August. He's never had a birthday party before."

"And you want me to what, make him a hat?" she asks.

"No, no," I tell her, "I wondered what you'd think of asking the store owners along Main Street if they'd be willing to ah . . . maybe . . . ah . . . if they'd . . . ah . . ."

"Ask them what, Gertie?" Her forehead's scrunched up. I can tell she wants me to get on with it.

So, I take a big breath and say it right out. "March in a community birthday parade for Sammy Stevens."

Her eyes pop open. "March in a *what*?"

"I know it sounds kinda funny," I say, "but the only birthday party Sammy wants is one with a parade. He got the idea from my birthday when we rode Jumbo the elephant in the circus parade."

Miss Clark pulls out a lace handkerchief and dabs it at her upper lip. "Well, Gertie," she says, "I certainly have nothing against Sammy Stevens. And I'm sure none of the other store owners do either. Except perhaps the butcher because of that Halloween chicken thing. But why on earth would any of them want to march in a community birthday parade for Sammy Stevens? Or anyone else for that matter?"

I know this is where I have to win her over, make her not just willing but wanting to help. So I fold my hands, kinda prayer-like, and start, "Because Richfield folks are caring folks. Because even store owners are caring neighbors first, then business folks who make their living off their neighbors. Because Jesus tells us that when we do something nice for somebody like Sammy, it's the same as doing something nice for Him. That's why."

I leave the millinery shop with Miss Ida Mae Clark's promise to talk to the other store owners to see if they'd be willing to help with a community parade! I'm so happy, I skip home singing, "*When we walk with the Lord in the light of His Word, what a glory He sheds on our way! While we do His good will He abides with us still, and with all who will trust and obey . . .*"

22

The List

HAVE YOU EVER HAD something go so good that you didn't bother to look at it hard to see if you missed anything? That's what happened to me. I'm so happy that Ida Mae Clark says she'll help, it's all I can think about. 'Til I tell Ella.

"Of course that is good news, Gertie," she says, "but it's only the beginning. We still have lots of plans to make. In fact, I've started a list. Like what's Sammy gonna ride in the parade? Are we gonna have music? Will there be birthday cake for everybody? Should we have balloons and paper streamers? How many blocks along Main Street should we march? Should we ask some of our friends, like the Teeter twins and Penny Peterson, to help? And what about me and you—what will we do in the parade?"

My head's goin' round and around. "Of course I know there's lots more plans to figure out," I tell her, and hope I sound more like I know what I'm doin' than I don't.

"Well?" she asks.

"Well what?" I ask back.

"Well, what *is* Sammy gonna ride in the parade? Really, Gertie, that's one of the most important things." She shakes her curls. "If we can't figure out something for him to lead the parade on, or in, or whatever, we might as well give up right now. We know it can't be an elephant. But it has to be something that'll make Sammy happy."

"How about a wagon?" I say.

Ella blows out a mouthful of air. "Now, Gertie, you know he's not gonna be happy riding in a wagon. Not after riding on Jumbo. It's gotta be something better than a rickety old wagon."

"I guess I could ask Aunt Danny if we could borrow Bossy," I try again.

Ella throws up her hands. "You don't mean her cow! Have you forgotten that day we rode her, and you ended up in an irrigation ditch, and I was bounced around on her back 'til I feared I'd be maimed for life?"

"Then I guess Wilson's bull isn't a good idea either," I say.

Ella pinches her mouth into a straight line. It's her "I'm disgusted!" look.

I grin. "I was only foolin'."

We stand there with our eyes glued on each other. I figure we're both wishing for the same thing: that somehow an idea will float out of somewhere and give us an answer. And that's the very thing that happens! Right at the same time we both say, "Mr. Hansen's mare, Jennie!"

"Well, Gertie," Ella says, "now at least we know what you'll be doing in the parade. You'll be riding Jennie with Sammy. Jenny knows you. You ride her pretty often. I bet Sammy's never been on a horse. Leastwise, not one as frisky as Jennie. First thing that'd happen is she'd buck him off. The only way we can be sure of Sammy staying on Jennie is for you to ride on her with him. And, Gertie, you'd better ask Mr. Hansen right away if you can borrow Jennie. Before we do any more planning, we need to know for certain that Sammy'll have something to ride on in his parade."

Since I have some time before I'm needed at the restaurant, I take off for the Hansen farm. When I get there, Mr. Hansen's sitting on his front porch. I'm wondering how to ask him 'bout borrowing Jennie for Sammy to ride. I figure it might be best to kinda sneak up on him with it. So, I say, "Hello, Mr. Hansen. How's Jennie?"

"Well, hello there, Gertie." He smiles at me. "Jennie's fine. Would you like to ride her? It's been awhile. You know you're always welcome to."

"No, thank you, Mr. Hansen," I tell him, "but I do have a favor to ask you. It's about Sammy Stevens."

He shakes his head and frowns. "Sammy Stevens?"

"Yes," I answer. "His papa's thinking of giving him a birthday party, the very first one Sammy's ever had. Mr. Stevens asked me to find out what kind of a party Sammy'd like. And you know what, Mr. Hansen, Sammy wants a party just like my last one! Can you believe that Sammy!"

"You don't mean with a circus parade?" he says, rubbing his forehead.

"Not exactly," I say. "But he does want a birthday parade."

"And you're telling me all this because . . ."

"Because Sammy'll need something to ride on in his parade," I tell him. "Course we can't rent an elephant. At first I thought of my Aunt Danny's cow, Bossy . . ."

"Wait a minute, Gertie," he cuts in, "are you trying to ask me if you can borrow Jennie for Sammy to ride in his birthday parade?"

"Well," I say, "I was. Sorta."

He shakes his head. "I'd like to help you, Gertie, but I don't think Sammy can handle Jennie. She's pretty lively, especially with someone she's not used to."

"If you let Sammy ride her, I'll ride her with him," I say. "I think she'll be fine with Sammy as long as I'm on her back, too."

"And when is this supposed to take place?" he asks

"Sometime 'round August 17th, Sammy's birthday," I answer.

He looks up at the sky like he's thinking. Or praying. Then he smiles. "Well, Gertie, if it was anyone but you, I'd say no. But you're always good with Jennie. And you're trustworthy. You never keep her longer than I say you can, and you always bring her back in good condition. I guess what I'm saying is, yes, you can borrow Jennie for Sammy to ride in his parade, especially since you'll be riding her with him."

"Thank you, Mr. Hansen! I promise to take good care of her." Then I tell him, "There's one more thing. Please don't say anything to anybody about this 'til I know for sure folks are willing to march in Sammy's parade. It'd be awful if Sammy heard he's having a birthday parade, and no one showed up to march in it. It would break his heart. That's been done enough times already, even by good folks who plain don't understand that Sammy's brain might not work right, but his heart beats as tender as anybody's." Mr. Hansen nods his head. I keep goin'. "If there are enough folks willing to march, I'll tell Sammy. If there aren't, he'll just miss out on another birthday party. And he won't even know it."

Mr. Hansen gives me one of those long looks grownups throw at you when they're trying to figure something out, either in their own brain or in yours. At last he says, "Tell you what, Gertie, you can count on me, the wife, and our two boys to march in Sammy's birthday parade. Yes, and our younger son's pet goat, Little Sis, too. Like the circus parade, it won't hurt to have a few wild animals following along."

I can hardly wait to tell Ella.

23

Time Out!

I T'S TOO NEAR SUPPER time to stop by Ella's with the good news about Jennie. I go straight to the restaurant to help with the customers. Later, I'm haulin' a tray of dirty dishes to the kitchen when I see Ella peeking in the front window. She stands there with a look on her face that asks, "What did Mr. Hansen say?" I nod and spread my mouth in the biggest grin I can, what with leftover bits of liver and onions just inches from my nose on the tray of dirty dishes I'm haulin'.

Ella jumps up and down. She mouths the words, "See you in the morning." Then she waves and skips up the street toward the funeral parlor.

When the supper rush is over, I'm tired and ready for bed. As I scrunch down between the covers, I hear Mama singing to Lorraine down the hall, *"Little birdie in the tree, in the tree, in the tree, little birdie in the tree sing a song for me . . ."* That's when Papa comes into the room to say goodnight.

"Don't forget to say your prayers," he calls to Pauline, who's just climbed in bed across the room.

"I won't, Papa," she calls back. She takes a wad of covers, pulls them up over her head, and begins to pray. Loud. So Papa will hear her.

He gives me a smile and a wink as if to say, "Isn't she the one!" Then he asks me, "Did you tell Mr. Stevens that Sammy wants a birthday party only if he can have a parade, too?"

"Not yet, Papa," I answer.

"Now, don't worry yourself sick over it, sweetheart. Sammy's never had a birthday party. He won't know what he's missing. There's just no way on earth that Mr. Stevens can come up with a parade."

When I don't say anything, his eyebrows jump. "Well, is there?"

"Actually," I say, "I came up with a community birthday parade idea. I even talked to a few folks to see if it might work. You know what, Papa? I already have a list of marchers started."

Papa's forehead folds into a frown. "A list of marchers?"

"Yes," I tell him, "I have four people signed up. And one goat."

"Well, I'll be!" Papa says. "Bet Mr. Stevens will be excited about that! Looks like you're handling things just fine."

That's when he switches from Sammy's birthday to something I'd just as soon he not switch to.

"Before I forget, Gertie," he says, switchin', "how's that bad tooth of yours? Been giving you any trouble lately?"

(Not many folks know about my sore tooth. Even when it's hurtin', they don't know about it. I don't want anybody telling me I have to go to the dentist. I tried that once. The dentist dabbed a little oil of cloves around the tooth, then started picking and digging into it. It hurt awful. I jumped out of the dentist chair, ran out the door, and down the street for home. I never went to the dentist again.)

"No, Papa," I tell him, "it hasn't bothered me for a long time. Why?"

He says, "I read in *The Richfield Reaper* that this Friday night some out-of-town dentists are putting on a demonstration at the community hall. They're going to fill and pull teeth free of charge. They claim they have some new kind of medicine that makes it all painless."

Painless? Ha! I don't believe it for a minute.

Wouldn't you know, that very night my tooth starts to ache, and ache awful. It feels like a sharp nail's poking me in the jaw. Poke! Poke! Poke!

On our way to school Tuesday morning, Ella wants to know all about my talk with Mr. Hansen. My tooth is still hurting. Bad. I don't feel like answering a bunch of her questions. But I don't want her to know why. So, I say I'm taking time out from Sammy's birthday party planning to tend to an important family matter that'll take a few days. I tell her it's a secret. Ella loves secrets. Even secrets that are kept secret from her.

With the pain in my tooth not letting up, I've 'bout decided to go to that tooth demonstration Friday night. If there's a chance my tooth can be fixed without it hurting any more than it's hurting now, I figure it might be worth looking into.

The next few days crawl by slow as snails. By Friday, I know for sure I'm going to that tooth demonstration. My tooth's still poking me awful. And keeping the pain to myself—even from Mama and Papa—makes it hurt all the more.

After school and chores, I tell Mama, "I'm thinking of going to that tooth demonstration at the community hall. Maybe I'll learn something that'll help me if my tooth ever bothers me again."

Mama thinks it's a good idea.

When it's time to leave, I head out the door. The rest of the family stays behind to clean-up. In the restaurant business there's always clean-up to do. Always.

By the time I get to the community hall, it's filling up fast. The folks who are finding seats must all have tooth troubles like me, I figure—folks who don't want to suffer any more at the hands of a dentist, no matter how well meaning he is. I find a chair on the aisle and slide onto it.

A tall, dark man is standing in the middle of the stage. He's dressed in a white jacket like our barber wears. And our butcher. And the clerk at the ice cream parlor.

"Welcome, ladies and gentlemen," he says. "My name is Dr. Walsworth, and I'm a dentist."

Right then, the muscles in my back knot up. Little drops, like dew, pop out on my upper lip and forehead.

"Yes, I'm a dentist," Dr. Walsworth is saying, "but believe it or not, you will discover this evening that I am also one of the best friends you will ever have!"

I peek at the folks around me. Many have the same look on their faces I know I have on mine. A look of hope.

"As was reported in your fine periodical, *The Richfield Reaper*, a wonderful new medicine has been developed called Novocain," he goes on. "It completely eliminates the pain that often accompanies dental work. Think of it, folks, no more pain in getting a tooth filled! No more pain in getting a tooth pulled! No more pain, period!"

There's some half-hearted clapping around the hall. You can tell folks want to believe this miracle but are afraid to.

"What I would like to do this evening is have a volunteer from the audience come up on stage. Someone with a current tooth problem. At no charge, I will pull or fill the troublesome tooth, and I guarantee it will be completely pain free! Do I have a volunteer?"

There's not a sound from anywhere in the hall. Not even a foot scraping. Not even a cough. Nothing.

"Now, come on folks, it's free and painless!" he says. "Surely someone will help me demonstrate the wonders of this new pain killing medicine."

A man down in front calls, "How do you give this new medicine, Doc?"

Dr. Walsworth answers, "We administer it through an injection into the gum using a hypodermic needle."

I hear shuffling at the back of the hall. I turn and look. A bunch of folks are tiptoeing for the door.

"Ladies and gentlemen," Dr. Walsworth is saying, "you're missing the point of this whole procedure. It is painless! You may feel a little pin prick when the Novocain is injected. But that's nothing to the pain I would venture some of you are feeling right now in a throbbing, aching tooth. Please, won't someone be brave enough to come up on stage and help me with my demonstration?"

Well, I've heard enough. My tooth is aching. I want to go home and go to bed. And that's what I make up my mind to do. Besides, I can tell nothing's gonna happen here. Everybody's glued to their seats. Except those folks who were smart enough to sneak out a few minutes ago.

I push back my chair and stand up. But before I can step into the aisle and head for the door, Dr. Walsworth raises a stiff arm and points it at me. "See! See! There's a young lady who's not a coward! Usher, please escort her to the stage. And, ladies and gentlemen, let's give her a big round of applause for her courage!"

I shake my head and try to tell 'em I'm just going home. But a strong hand grabs my elbow and pulls me into the aisle and down toward the stage. I call up to Dr. Walsworth that I'm not volunteering. But it's so noisy with everybody clapping, and some folks calling, "Atta girl, Gertie!"

"You show 'em, Gertie!"

"We're with you, Gertie!" that he doesn't hear me. Leastwise, he acts like he doesn't.

Before I know it, I'm dragged up the stairs onto the stage and pushed into a chair. I try to get up, but a lady dressed in that same white jacket slings a towel 'round my neck and ties it in the back. Then she grabs onto the towel and holds me in place.

While the crowd cheers on, Dr. Walsworth pries my mouth open. He takes a wicked looking thing, like a little metal hammer, and taps it on each of my teeth. When he gets to my bad tooth, I jump a foot and let out a yelp!

"Aha," he says to the noisy crowd, "I've found the culprit. It's a permanent tooth. I'll clean out the decay and fill it with a nice silver filling." Then he picks up another wicked looking thing, this one with a long needle sticking out the end, and aims it at my mouth.

I feel like I'm gonna be sick.

24

Time In!

I CAN'T TELL IT good enough. But I'll try. My scared feelings melt away as the Novocain Dr. Walsworth sticks in my gum makes my mouth go numb. After a couple of minutes, my tooth doesn't hurt at all.

I want to tell him I don't need my tooth filled now; that it doesn't hurt anymore. But my mouth won't work. It keeps droolin', and my tongue won't do what I want it to.

"Now, relax, Gertie," he tells me, "this isn't going to hurt." And you know what? It doesn't! Before I know it, the hole in my tooth is cleaned out and filled with silver!

"All right, young lady, we're all through," Dr. Walsworth says. "Now, I want you to please tell the audience, did you feel any pain after I gave you the Novocain?"

I swallow a couple of times, but my mouth keeps drippin' and my tongue keeps floppin'. All I can do is shake my head back and forth.

The whole hall starts cheering and clapping again! It truly is a great day for folks with bad teeth.

Later, when I get home, I tell Mama and Papa all that happened. They hug and kiss me. Then off to bed we go, rejoicing and praising God for Novocain, with a kind word or two for Dr. Walsworth.

The next morning, the news of my "volunteering" gets around Richfield in a hurry. Everybody who comes into the restaurant says I'm a hero.

"Thanks to you, Gertie, now we can go to the dentist without fear of pain." The lady talking is one I saw at the demonstration last night. She was stretched out in her chair with her head hanging over the back. Some man was fanning her with her bonnet. Whatever was bothering her then, doesn't seem to be bothering her now. She's gobbling down a breakfast of sausage, eggs, fried potatoes, and flapjacks.

When Ella hears 'bout me having my tooth filled in front of all those folks, which I figure was 'bout seventy or more, she comes hurrying into the restaurant.

"Do you see what this is gonna do for our community birthday parade?" she fairly shouts at me.

"What?" I ask her.

"Well, who's gonna say 'No' to you now when you ask them to march in Sammy's parade? Don't you hear what folks are saying about you? That you, a little ten-year-old girl, were the only person in that whole hall who had the courage to stand up and volunteer to be part of the Novocain demonstration. Everybody else was too scared. If you hadn't been willing, we might never have seen the proof of the miracle of Novocain." She closes her eyes and bows her head, like in church.

I feel awful. I know in my heart that when I stood up it wasn't to volunteer. It was to run for home.

That night I can't sleep. I keep wondering, what shall I do? Should I tell them I didn't volunteer? That I was afraid like everybody else? That I wanted to run for home? That I'm no hero? The next morning in Sunday School, I get an answer to my questions. And I didn't even think to pray for one.

Sometimes it happens that way. Sometimes God steps in and helps even when we don't get around to asking Him to. That's the kind of God He is.

Mr. Tannehill starts class by telling the children about my part in the Novocain demonstration, in case anybody hasn't heard. A couple of bratty boys keep "oohing" and "ahhing" in a smarty pants way. Like it's news to them. I'm about to stand up and say I didn't volunteer, partly to shut 'em up, partly because it's the truth. But Mr. Tannehill says something that stops me right in my tracks.

"What happened to Gertie illustrates how God works through the events of our lives to perform His will, which in this case was to bless His children. Especially those with bad teeth. I'm sure when Gertie went to that demonstration Friday night, she had no idea the Lord was going to use her to help others." He throws me a big smile. "Now, I don't mean to take anything away from Gertie's bravery, but I hope you children see that the real importance of what happened is not that Gertie volunteered. It's that God worked it all out, and would have even if she hadn't volunteered. Why do I say this? Because it's obvious with the development of Novocain that

God does not want His children to suffer from toothaches anymore." He puts his hand to his jaw and rubs it hard. Like he's thinking of something painful that happened to him. "While we can thank Gertie for her part in the demonstration, we must remember that God is sovereign. He is in control. He is the One worthy of our praise and gratitude." Mr. Tannehill throws me another smile. "Am I right, Gertie? Do you give God the credit for what happened at the Novocain demonstration?"

Relief floods my soul. "Amen!" I shout.

On the way home, Ella scolds me. "I don't know why you let Mr. Tannehill take all of the glory away from you. Of course, it's fine to give God some of the credit. But you're the one who has to talk folks into joining Sammy's community birthday parade. Not God. If folks don't feel like they owe you something, it'll be easy for them to say no."

But I don't see it that way. If God worked it all out, like Mr. Tannehill said He did, then He must have known folks would think I'm a hero and be willing to march in Sammy's parade. It means God's happy we're having a parade! Now it's up to me and Ella to find a way to tell Sammy's father so he'll be happy about it, too.

25

Yes!

AS BEST AS I can remember, it's Wednesday, late afternoon, when Mr. Stevens comes into the restaurant for supper. He's alone. Sammy, he tells me, is spending the evening with Widow Gustafson and her family. Which kinda surprises me. Sammy doesn't go visiting same as other folks do. Then he says, "Widow Gustafson's dog, Molly, has a new litter of pups." I'm not kinda surprised anymore.

There's only a few early supper eaters, so I'm not too busy. I scrape back the chair next to his, and slide onto it. He asks me if I've talked to Sammy yet 'bout having a birthday party. I tell him I have.

"And yes, sir," I say, "I think he'd like to have a party."

"Well, good!" he says.

"But," and I suck in a breath so big, my shoulders end up under my ears, "only if he can have one like my last birthday."

I can fairly see the wheels going 'round and around inside his brain. "You don't mean with a circus parade?!" he says.

"Yes, sir, well no, sir, not exactly. I don't think it has to be a circus parade. As best as I can figure, Sammy just wants a parade—a birthday parade."

That's when Ella skips through the door, curls bouncin', skirt flouncin', and plunks herself down at our table. Quick like I tell Mr. Stevens that if Sammy has a party, Ella says she's willing to help. "She's known for her parties, Mr. Stevens. She has lots of good ideas."

Ella tips her head to one side, looks down at her folded hands, bats her eyelashes, and tries to look humble. It doesn't work.

"I appreciate that you talked to Sammy, Gertie, and that you're willing to help with his party. You, too, Ella. But I guess it doesn't matter now." Mr. Stevens shakes his head. "There's no way in the world we can manage a parade for Sammy's birthday."

I figure now is the time to tell him the good news. "Actually, Mr. Stevens, me and Ella think there's a good chance we can have a birthday parade for Sammy. We've even started a list . . ."

"A list?" Mr. Stevens cuts in. His eyelids blink open and shut. He shakes his head, and gives his forehead a good rub. "What do you mean, 'a list'?"

"Well," I say, "when I went to the Hansen farm to ask Mr. Hansen if Sammy can ride his mare, Jennie, in the parade . . ."

Mr. Stevens holds up his hand like he wants to cut in again. "You asked Mr. Hansen if Sammy can ride his horse?"

"Yes, sir, and he says he can," I tell him. "He says he and his wife and two sons and their pet goat will be marchers, too. So, we started a list."

Mr. Stevens blinks his eyes, shakes his head, and rubs his forehead some more.

That's when Ella takes over. I was afraid she would. But I need her to help, so I just let her go. "A parade is very possible, Mr. Stevens. Certainly, it will take a bit of doing, but I've been planning birthday parties for years. I'm sure we can put on a parade." Then she nods her curly head at me. "Gertie, please tell Mr. Stevens about your talk with Miss Ida Mae Clark."

"Well," I say, "we thought if we got the store owners along Main Street to see that a parade could be good for business . . ."

Mr. Stevens holds up his hand again. "How in the world can a birthday parade for Sammy be good for Main Street business?" He does some more of that blinkin', shakin', and rubbin'.

As soon as he settles down, I say, "It would show folks that store owners aren't just out to make a living off the community; that they're good neighbors who care about the Richfield folks they're out to make a living off of." The corners of his mouth twitch, like he's fighting off a smile or feeling sick. I can't tell which. I go on, "Miss Ida Mae Clark thinks it's a good idea. She's gonna talk to the other store owners about it."

"Well," he says, "that's quite a plan you've come up with. But what if there're not enough folks willing to make up a parade? If Sammy thinks he's having a parade, then there aren't enough folks willing to march in it, he'll be awfully disappointed."

"You needn't worry, Mr. Stevens," Ella takes over again, "we're not saying a word about this to Sammy until we're sure of our plan. We're asking everybody else to do the same."

Mr. Stevens says. "Well, I wouldn't want to stand in the way . . ."

"Good!" says Ella, "Then it's settled. We'll have a birthday parade for Sammy. And don't worry, Mr. Stevens, we'll take care of everything. The music. The birthday cakes. Everything. I checked the calendar this morning. August 17th comes on a Sunday. We better have Sammy's birthday parade on the 16th so as not to upset all the preachers in town. We can gather at Fourth Street and march up Main Street to the Baptist Church. That's three blocks. Their Fellowship Hall is perfect for serving the birthday cakes. Oh, and I asked Mr. Dennis to help with the dust problem. He says he'll hitch Old Ben to his water wagon and spray the street before the parade starts." She taps her fingers on the table, important-like. "We should start the parade no later than ten o'clock in the morning. That way we'll avoid the heat of the day."

Mr. Stevens looks like what Aunt Danny calls "overwhelmed." That means, well actually I don't know what it means, but it seems to fit Mr. Stevens. He stands up and sort of stumbles toward the door, bumping into a table or two along the way. I figure he's forgot 'bout supper, or isn't as hungry as he thought he was. Anyway, once out the door, he turns right, stops, rubs his forehead, then turns left and weaves out of sight.

"Hummm," says Ella, "I think that went very well." She digs in the pocket of her dress and pulls out a sheet of paper with lots of writing on it. Then digs around some more for a pencil. "Let's see, we got a big 'Yes!' from Mr. Stevens on our parade idea. *Check*. Miss Ida Mae Clark says she'll talk to the other business owners. *Check*. Mr. Hansen says Sammy can ride Jennie in the parade. *Check*. Mr. Dennis will drive his water wagon up the street to help keep the dust down. *Check*." Each time she says, "check," she makes a mark with her pencil next to the thing on her list she's checking. "That leaves the birthday cakes, Baptist Church, music, decorations, and you—our tooth hero—to talk folks into being marchers." She rolls her eyes toward the ceiling and chews on her pencil. "Can you think of anything else, Gertie?"

I'm sorry to have to tell her I can't. But I make up my mind right then that I will think of something else. And I won't tell her what. It'll be a surprise. Something she can't claim as her idea or butt into. I don't know what it'll be, but it'll be something.

That night, when Papa comes to tuck me and Pauline into bed, I tell him about my talk—I mean me and Ella's talk—with Mr. Stevens.

Papa asks, "So, Mr. Stevens wants you to go ahead with the parade idea?"

"Yes, Papa," I tell him.

"Gertie, I'm awful proud of you," he says, "and Ella, too, of course. If there's anything Mama and I can do to help, just let us know."

"Maybe Mama can bake a cake or two. We're gonna need lots," I tell him.

"I'm sure she'll be happy to." He reaches down and plants a goodnight kiss on my forehead. Then he puts one hand on his chest, sticks his other arm out to the side, and dips and sways his way across the room to Pauline.

When she sees him waltzing her way, she giggles. "Oh, Papa!"

I have to say, it's a wonder my folks have any zip left after working so hard in our restaurant all day. I figure they must save some just for us. Like right now I can hear Mama singing to Lorraine down the hall, *"Oh the cat chased the kitten and the kitten chased the pup, and they ran around the table with their tails a-stickin' up . . . "* Guess that's what it means to be a mama or a papa—save enough of yourself each day to have some zip left to play with your children. That's something I'm gonna remember when I'm a mama or a papa. I mean a mama.

26

Plans, Plans, And More Plans

BY THE TIME SAMMY's birthday's just two weeks away, we have over thirty marchers! And the list keeps growin'! Me and Ella figure it's time to tell Sammy 'bout his birthday parade. Of course he bawls when we tell him the news. We know he's happy, though, with all the teeth and gum that's showing along with his tears.

"What about Jumbo?" he finally stops bawling long enough to ask.

"Do you mean the elephant or your dog?" Ella wants to know.

"I mean my dog," he answers.

"Well, what about him?" Ella asks.

"I asked you first," Sammy says.

Ella snaps her head. "Are we gonna stand here wasting time playing this silly game of who asked who what first?"

I figure I better step in before she gets too riled. "Sammy, are you asking if Jumbo, *your dog,* is gonna be in your parade?"

He drags his sleeve across his watery eyes. "Yes, Gertie."

"Well, of course he is," I tell him. "Pauline's gonna pull Jumbo in her little red wagon right behind you riding on Mr. Hansen's mare, Jennie."

I guess I should've done more to ready him for that bit of news. He looks like he's gonna be sick. "I never rode a horse before, Gertie. Just a elephant."

"Well, don't worry, Sammy," Ella tells him, "Gertie's gonna ride with you so Jennie won't buck you off."

She maybe means to comfort him, but her "buck you off" just turns him a shade whiter. It takes me awhile to calm him down. Poor Sammy.

"We've asked the Teeter twins to lead off your parade playing your favorite song," I tell him. "Their papa's gonna fix their new piano on the back of his wagon. It's an American Home Upright Parlor Grand Piano he ordered from the Sears, Roebuck & Company catalogue for $98.50. He says he's proud and happy for his girls to play for the parade. (Mostly, I figure, to show off his new piano. Leastwise, he brags about it enough.)

Sammy blows out a big sigh. He plainly needs time to think this all over. "When you come up with the song you'd like the twins to play, let me know," I tell him.

"All right, Gertie," he says.

Later that day, I'm heading up the street to the restaurant. I look up at the balcony outside my bedroom. Sometimes Mary or Pauline wait for me there—mostly to yell at me to hurry up so I can help with chores. Nobody's there now. But that's when the idea for the big surprise I'm hoping to come up with comes up.

Remember how I was gonna put on a circus of my own for my tenth birthday party activity? One of the circus tricks I planned was a parachute jump from that balcony. Course I was gonna use Papa's umbrella, not a real parachute. I figure since I didn't use the trick then, I can use it now as the big surprise for Sammy's birthday parade! We won't jump from the balcony, though. That would hold up the parade too long. We need a place to jump at the end of the parade when everybody's stopped. And I know just the place. The church bell tower!

All we need is the jumper. Somebody who can be up in the bell tower when the parade pulls into the church yard. Then at a signal, a loud chord on the piano by the Teeter twins, the jumper will open the umbrella and jump. It will be a wonderful surprise ending to the parade. I can hardly wait to see Ella's mouth hang open and her eyes bug out when the surprise hits her!

First, though, I have to find somebody to jump. One of the bratty boys will do it, I figure. They love to show off.

There's an old saying, "You can try, you can hope, you can almost choke, but don't count on a bratty boy, he's bound to tell you 'Nope!'" Actually, I made that up. Sad to say, the next couple of days, my old saying proves true. Every time I hunt down a big tough bratty boy and ask him to be the jumper, every bratty one of them says the same thing, "Are you crazy? I could break a leg!" So, it appears there'll be no big surprise at the end of Sammy's parade after all. I'm glad I didn't tell Ella what I was planning.

Then on Tuesday, just four days before the parade, something wonderful happens. I get another idea. Actually, it's more like a vision. Not a vision of angels like you read about in the Bible. But just 'bout as good.

It's late afternoon. I'm on my way back from the spillway getting another bucket of water for Mama. Who should I see but Penny Peterson and her pet duck, Ruthie, waddling up the street. Penny takes Ruthie for a walk most every day on a leash. Ruthie's a nice enough duck, though she does get frisky at times. All at once, Ruthie jumps into the air. She flaps her wings and flies a few feet. That's when I get my vision—a vision of Ruthie parachuting out of the church bell tower!

Penny's very proud of her duck. It doesn't take me long to talk her into letting Ruthie be the big star of the big surprise. "But, Gertie, how's Ruthie gonna hold onto the umbrella?" Penny asks me.

"I just figured that out," I tell her. "We'll ask my friend, Miss Ida Mae Clark, to make Ruthie a harness to wear. We'll tie the harness to the umbrella."

The more we talk about it, the better it sounds. Penny will carry Ruthie up into the bell tower when the parade starts. She'll feed Ruthie some grain to keep her happy. Then when she sees the parade a block away, she'll slip Ruthie into her harness. When the parade gets to the church yard, and the Teeter twins give the signal on their piano, Penny will open the umbrella and toss it out of the bell tower with Ruthie, in her harness, hanging from it.

"Oh, Gertie, Ruthie floating in the air with everybody watching and cheering, I can just see it," Penny tells me.

"Yes," I say, "I can just see it, too."

27

Getting It All Together

Aftfter we drop off the bucket of water I got for Mama at the spillway, me, Penny, and Ruthie head for Ida Mae Clark's millinery shop. With only four days 'til Sammy's birthday parade, we can't waste any time if Miss Clark is to get a harness ready for Ruthie to wear.

Miss Clark is her pinchy, patty, squeezy self. Before I can say why we've come, she pinches my nose, pats my head, and gives me a squeeze. Then she heads for Penny and Ruthie.

When Ruthie sees her comin', she stretches her head to one side, turns a big eye on Miss Clark, and raises her wings like a boxer ready to fight. Sad to say, Miss Clark pays her no mind. She grabs a handful of Penny's cheek. That's when Ruthie lets out a squawk and nips Miss Clark on the leg.

Lucky for us, it's not a bad bite, and Miss Clark's a good sport. She's smart enough, too, not to pinch us any more, which suits me fine.

When things settle down, I tell her, "We have a favor to ask of you, Miss Clark."

She pulls up her skirt a bit and rubs a red spot on her leg. "I suppose it has to do with the community parade on Saturday?"

"Yes, ma'am," I say. "We're planning a big surprise at the end of the parade. You, me, and Penny are the only ones who'll know about it."

"*Really?*" she says, smiling and patting the waves of hair lapping over her ears.

I hurry on. "Yes. We're gonna have a surprise parachute jump from the church bell tower when the parade marches into the church yard. We'll use my papa's umbrella as the parachute."

"Oh, my, that will be a big surprise," she says. "Who's the brave jumper?"

"Well," I say, "that kinda depends on you ..."

She throws up her hands. "Now, wait a minute, Gertie, you don't think for a moment that I'll ..."

"No, no! I just mean we need you to help our jumper jump," I tell her.

"How in the world am I to do that?" She reaches inside the sleeve of her dress, pulls out her lace handkerchief and pats it across her upper lip.

"We need you to make a harness for our jumper to wear that can be fixed to the parachute," I say.

"May I inquire again who the brave jumper is?" she asks.

That's when Penny speaks up, proud as a peacock, "My pet duck, Ruthie!"

Miss Clark covers her mouth with her handkerchief. Her head flops back and forth. She makes a sort of choking sound. I'm wondering if she swallowed a bug which is pretty common this time of year with all the gnats and flies in the air. After a minute or two she calms down.

"I'll be happy to sew a harness for Ruthie," she says, "I wouldn't miss being a part of this for anything!"

We get her to promise she won't tell anyone. "No, no, I'll keep your surprise. I mean *our* surprise."

The next couple of minutes are like a wrestling match with me and Penny holding a wiggling, flapping, squawking Ruthie while Miss Clark measures her for a harness. We all end up with a nip here and there, but none of us bleed any amount worth mentioning.

Miss Clark says she'll have the harness ready the next day, Thursday. Penny is to pick it up on her way home from school. Only one little thing worries me. With school and chores and all, there won't be time to try things out before the parade.

The next two days fly by. Penny tells me she picked up the harness from Miss Clark. It fits Ruthie fine. Cakes are being baked and hauled to the Baptist Church. Some store owners have decorated their front windows, some have made signs to carry in the parade, some have done both. All over town, folks are calling to each other, "See you at Sammy's parade Saturday!" It's plain to me that God's answering my prayer. I asked Him to bless Sammy's first birthday party and parade, and He's using the good Richfield folks to do just that. Thank You, God.

Then the night before the parade, me, Aunt Danny, Grandpa and Grandma Larson, Mama, Papa, Mary, and Pauline are sitting around the kitchen table. Lorraine's already been tucked in bed. The supper customers have come and gone. The dirty dishes are washed and put away. The *"Closed"* sign is set in the front window.

Grandma Larson says, "Why don't we say a prayer for Sammy's parade? Gertie and Ella have worked hard for weeks arranging everything. It's like a miracle how many of the business owners and other folks are willing to join in."

"That's a good idea, Cloe," Grandpa says, and reaches out for us to join hands 'round the table. "Dear Lord," he begins, "lots of work's gone into planning Sammy's community birthday parade. Please bless him with a birthday he will always remember. And bless all those who've worked so hard to make it happen. Amen." Then he pulls out the little Bible he carries in his back pocket, and opens it. "I thought this would be a good verse to think on tonight. It's from the Book of Philippians, Chapter 4, verses 6 and 7." He takes a big breath and starts to read, "'Be careful for nothing, but in everything by prayer and supplication with thanksgiving let your requests be made known to God. And the peace of God, which passeth all understanding, shall keep your hearts and minds through Christ Jesus.'"

Grandpa looks at me. "I know the weight of Sammy's parade coming off well is resting heavy on you, Gertie. But since we've asked our Lord to give the parade His blessing, and we have the promise of this Bible verse, you don't have to carry that heavy burden any longer. You can rest easy now."

I go to bed that night excited and happy. Tomorrow is the big parade. I can hardly wait. I wonder if I'll ever get to sleep. And that's the last thought I think 'til I wake up the next morning. Grandpa's prayer worked!

28

Sammy's Community Birthday Parade!

SATURDAY MORNING'S WILD AND wooly. But not everywhere. Just at the corner of Fourth and Main where the parade's lining up. Even Ella with her pencil and list can't calm things down. Check.

Jumbo keeps poppin' out of his wagon and running around looking for Sammy. Two bratty boys think it's more fun to wrestle in the street than to march in it. The ladies of the poetry society, *Spending Time In Rhyme,* don't like their place in line. Ella put them in front of Mr. Hansen's family and pet goat, Little Sis. It's Little Sis the poetry ladies don't cater to. She keeps munching the lilacs and roses pinned to their sign: *Birthday Joy to the Birthday Boy!*

Ella's near to tears. "Let's pray," I tell her. We don't have much time, only enough for a quick, "Please help us, Lord." But we both feel better.

Just then, someone pats me on the shoulder. I turn. There stands Sammy. His face is lit up like a sparkler. If I ever wondered if all the work and worry goin' into this day was worth it, I don't wonder any longer.

"I'm here, Gertie," he tells me.

"Yes, you are, Sammy, and a big Happy Birthday to you!"

I look around. I see Mr. Teeter is driving his wagon into place at the head of the parade. The twins are at the American Home Upright Parlor Grand piano. Just then, Mr. Hansen brings Jennie, all brushed and curried, and hands me the reins. She tosses her main and paws her hoof on the ground, like she knows she's beautiful.

"Have a great parade," Mr. Hansen tells Sammy, then goes to join his family and goat in the parade line.

I figure I'll wait to get me and Sammy up onto Jennie's back 'til we're ready to start the parade. From the looks of things, it won't be long now. The bratty boys have settled down. Thank You, Lord! Jumbo is back in his wagon with Pauline standing guard. Thank You, Lord! And the poetry ladies are happy. Ella found them a place in line away from Little Sis and her taste for fresh flowers. Thank You, Lord!

As the marchers come and slip into line, some are carrying signs. Mr. Cavnar's sign has printing on both sides. One side says, *"Meat is the bread of life. Come to Canvar's and try a slice! (Free soup bones while they last.)"* The other side says, *"Happy Birthday, Sammy, from Cavnar's Butcher Shop."*

Mr. Tannehill's sign is an invitation to join his class. *"Come to Sunday School at the Baptist Church and learn about God before it is too late. Happy Birthday, Sammy!"*

Mary made our sign with pictures of food 'round the edge—slices of cake, bowls of soup, pot roast, baked chicken. It makes my stomach grumble just to look at it.

All at once, Ella comes running from somewhere down the line of marchers. "People are getting restless, Gertie. We better start the parade." She whirls and runs back, waving and yelling, "It won't be long now!"

I take hold of Sammy's arm. "We'd better get up on Jennie," I tell him. "Your parade's about to start."

That's when one of the folks watching from the sidewalk yells, "Look, there's Gertie! How's that tooth, Gertie?" Then somebody else yells, "That's Gertie, the volunteer at the Novocain demonstration. Hi, Gertie!"

All at once it comes over me. Here it is Sammy's big day, and who's getting most of the attention? Me. In a way, it's nice. But this is Sammy's parade. He's the one who should get the attention. I make up my mind right then, Sammy'll ride Jennie alone. I'll walk beside her holding the reins. I figure she'll be fine as long as I'm by her side, patting and cooing her along. Maybe that way folks won't notice me so much.

"Gertie! Gertie!" Miss Ida Mae Clark rushes up to me. "I'm sorry I'm late. Do you want me just anywhere in line?" She's carrying a pole with seven or eight of her straw hats and bonnets hanging from it. It gives me an idea.

"Can I wear that green checkered bonnet in the parade?" I ask her.

She smiles, and pats my face. "Of course, Gertie, and thank you for advertising my chapeau." (I find out later that "chapeau" is French for bonnet.) She hands me the bonnet, then skips along the marchers 'til she finds a place in line to her liking.

As fast as I can, I pull the bonnet down over my hair and tuck my braids inside. Now it'll be hard for folks to tell who I am and yell at me instead of at Sammy. Then I cup my hands and give Sammy a hand-up onto Jennie's back, with the help of a kind watcher from the sidewalk.

I take a quick peek up and down the line of marchers. It's a beautiful, wonderful sight. There are store owners, farmers, Miss Goldbranson and a few other teachers, some boys and girls from my class at school, a preacher or two, Doc Summers and his missus in their horse and buggy, mamas and papas with their little ones, some dogs, cats, and a chicken or two, a few bratty boys, and Hansen's goat. Bringing up the rear is Widow Gustafson and her girls pulling a wagon totin' a box full of wigglin' puppies. On one side of the box is printed, *"Free puppies to loving homes."* On the other side, *"Happy Birthday Dear Sammy!"*

I look up at Sammy. "Are you ready for your big birthday parade?"

"Yes, Gertie," he says, and blows out a happy sigh.

I'm happy, too, seeing him so content up there on Jennie's back alone.

Mr. Teeter and the twins are watching for my signal to start. I give them a big arm wave. Mr. Teeter guides his wagon into the middle of the street. Tilly and Lilly begin to pound away on their new piano. The notes of Sammy's favorite song tell the marchers and the folks waiting along the sidewalk that the parade's startin'!

"For goodness sake, Gertie, that's Sammy's favorite song? That's what he chose for us to march to? 'Onward Christian Soldiers'?" Ella's skipping along beside me now.

"Yes," I tell her, "that's Sammy's favorite song. That's what he wanted, and that's what he's gettin.'"

Ella doesn't say any more. Actually, she starts singing along with the twins' playing, *". . . with the cross of Jesus going on before . . . "*

Block after block, the folks along the sidewalk wave and cheer us on. I'm glad they mostly wave and yell at Sammy. "Happy birthday, Sammy!"

"Ride 'em cowboy!"

"Atta boy, Sammy!"

He waves and yells back, "It's my birthday parade!" He's smiling like I've never seen him smile before.

It takes nearly an hour to march the three blocks to the Baptist Church. Leastwise, that's how long it seems. When we're all in the church yard, I get up on Mr. Teeter's wagon and put up both hands for folks to be quiet. "Thank you for marching in Sammy's community birthday parade," I tell them. I have to stop while they cheer and clap for themselves. "Before we go inside the Fellowship Hall for birthday cake, we have a big surprise for you. Would you all please look up at the church bell tower." I give the twins a wave. They hit a loud chord on the piano.

Everybody turns and looks up. I can see Penny wrestling with Ruthie to get her in her harness. Just as I'm wondering if I'll have to climb the tower stairs to help her, out from the bell tower shoots the umbrella with Ruthie, in her harness, dangling from it.

Everybody points and goes "Oooooooo!"

It truly is a beautiful sight—Ruthie with her snow colored wings stretched out wide, and Papa's umbrella with its black silk panels shimmering in the sunlight. Slowly the umbrella floats higher like a feather caught on the morning breeze.

Everybody points and goes "Ahhhhhhh!"

Ella's watching with her mouth hanging open, just like I knew she would. She's a beautiful sight, too.

Then all at once, Ruthie starts wigglin' 'round in her harness. She pokes and picks at it with her beak. The umbrella dips and sways. Instead of floating higher like a feather, it heads for the ground like a leaky balloon. That's when Ruthie slips out of her harness and takes off over the bell tower.

Everybody points and goes "Loooooook!"

The last we see of Ruthie, she's headed north toward Salt Lake City, flapping her wings for all she's worth.

29

Figuring It All Out

It's a puzzle how different folks see the same thing different. Like some of the folks think Ruthie's slipping out of her harness and flying off over the bell tower is part of the surprise. They wave and cheer her on. Poor Penny grabs a wad of her face in each hand and starts to cry. And Ella? Well, the way she takes it is the biggest puzzle of all.

Ruthie is barely out of sight when Ella throws her arms around me. Her eyes are watery. I figure it's 'cause she feels bad Ruthie's flying off. But it's far from that.

"Oh, Gertie," she cries, "that's the most beautiful thing you've ever done!"

I wiggle loose from her arms. "How in the world can Penny losing her precious Ruthie be 'beautiful'?" I ask.

"You gave that poor wild creature its freedom, that's what I mean," she answers. "Every time I saw Penny draggin' Ruthie around on that dog leash, I just cringed. If she wants a pet, she can get a cat!"

Four days later, a miracle happens. Ruthie comes waddlin' into Penny's front yard! She looks awful. Some of her feathers are bent, some broken, some gone. Course she can't say where she's been or what's happened to her. But it's plain to see, smell actually, that somewhere along the way her little webbed feet led her into a field covered with fresh manure. But Penny doesn't care. She's so happy to have Ruthie back home, she even starts talking to me again.

By now the excitement of Sammy's parade is mostly over. Oh, everybody still talks about it. Says it was a wonderful parade. Mr. Stevens is so grateful to us parade marchers that he invites us to a special noon get-together at the Baptist Church the following Saturday.

"After I give my little appreciation talk," he tells us, "we'll move into the Fellowship Hall for a delicious dinner of fried chicken and all the trimmings!"

When Saturday arrives, most everybody who marched in the parade turns up at the church. Course no goats, or chickens, or dogs, or cats, or horses turn up. Only grownups and children.

When it looks like everybody that's coming is come, Mr. Stevens says, "I want to thank each one of you for your kindness to my son, Sammy. I especially want to thank Gertie and Ella for working so hard to put on that wonderful birthday parade." He stops while the folks clap. "And Mr. Teeter and his talented twins for the wonderful music we marched to." More clapping. "And the ladies who baked the birthday cakes." Lots more clapping. "And Leona Gustafson for arranging with Preacher Brown to use the Fellowship Hall today."

As the folks clap some more, I look around for Widow Gustafson. But I don't see her anywhere. I wonder why.

"Now Sammy wants to thank you himself," Mr. Stevens is saying. He gives Sammy a pat and a push.

Sammy dips his head down and looks up through the tops of his eyeballs, shy like.

"Thanks, folks," he says, "and thank you, Gertie. You're my best friend."

His papa whispers something in his ear. "Oh, and thank you, too, Ella," he says.

Then Mr. Stevens tells us, "Now, we have a big surprise for you, dear friends. No, it has nothing to do with Penny Peterson's pet duck parachuting out of the church bell tower!" Everybody laughs and claps some more. "We got you here a bit under false pretenses," he goes on. "Yes, we wanted to thank you. But we also wanted you to be present at the joining together of the Stevens and Gustafson families in holy matrimony."

One big "gasp!" bounces back and forth along the pews.

Mrs. Summers, who must be in on the surprise, slides onto the piano bench. She raises her hands a foot above the keys and bangs them down on the first chords of "Onward Christian Soldiers." In through the big double doors and down the aisle march Widow Gustafson and her three daughters, Emily Rose, Nancy Iris, and Hannah Floret.

Well, it turns out to be one of the most beautiful weddings ever. Leastwise, that's what everybody says. Prob'ly 'cause of all the huggin' and kissin' that goes on after Preacher Brown raises his hand and says, "I now pronounce you husband, wife, and family." Well, I'm thinkin', that ends the ceremony. But that's not what Preacher Brown's thinkin'. He's thinkin' he has something more to say. I truly believe preachers can't miss a chance to preach. It's just not in 'em to let a chance slip by. But what he says makes me happy he says it. Anyway, it's short.

"Before we go into the Fellowship Hall to partake of that delicious fried chicken we've been smelling, I want to share a few thoughts with Mr. and Mrs. Stevens." He holds up his Bible. "As I read in Genesis 2:24 during the ceremony, 'Therefore shall a man leave his father and his mother, and shall cleave unto his wife, and they shall be one flesh.' We can't hear it often enough that it was God who first brought man and woman together in holy matrimony. It's His purpose. His design." He cuddles his Bible against his chest and keeps on talking, "This is a second marriage for you both— both of you having lost a mate through death. How good is our Lord to give you to each other so you won't have to live out your lives alone. And what a joy it is for your children to have both a papa and a mama to love and care for them." That's when Sammy grins so hard, I fear his face will cramp. And that's when Widow Gustafson—I mean Mrs. Stevens—hugs him so tight, I fear she'll choke him.

At last, Preacher Brown stops his preaching and says the blessing for the food we're 'bout to eat. As soon as he gets to the "Amen!", we push and shove our way into the Fellowship Hall and up to the tables loaded with fried chicken and all the trimmings.

If you're figuring those platters of chicken, bowls of potato salad, mounds of homemade bread, hunks of watermelon, and three-layered wedding cake heaped high with frosting, are the end to my third real life adventure, you're figuring right. Now I'm lookin' for my next real life adventure to come along. I can hardly wait!

I learned a lot this past year 'bout how God uses our adventures to teach us things. One thing He taught me is that a real life adventure can be like a flat rock skipping across the pond of life. Just when you think it's 'bout to sink, it skips and splashes along some more. Like the Stevens and Gustafson wedding skipping and splashing along behind Sammy's birthday parade. Another thing He taught me is that the best adventures of all are the ones we share with family and friends—that it's mostly the sharing that makes an adventure best. God taught me, too, sad to say, that adventures can have some troublesome parts. Like being told you can't have a birthday party, or like losing your puppy, or like being sick and having to sleep in a teepee. But, happy to say, God promises to help us through the troublesome parts if we ask Him to. He's always waiting to hear our voice 'cause He loves us and wants to help us when we call on Him. (Remember how I prayed for a birthday activity? And for Sammy to get Jumbo back? And for Little Moon Wind to get well?)

Oh, oh, Mary's yelling at me to load the dirty dishes onto a tray and get 'em into the kitchen. But before I do, I want to ask you, did you like my adventures? Maybe me and you can share a real life adventure someday. Don't forget, you never know when one's gonna pop up.

There she goes hollerin' at me again! Sounds like she means business.

"Hold your horses, Mary, I'm comin'."

Well, I gotta go. Sorry I gotta say goodbye. But there's an old saying, "A goodbye to a friend is like a prayer of your heart that you'll soon meet again and not long be apart." Actually, I made that up. But it's true just the same. So, 'though I'm sorry I gotta say it, I'll say it—like a prayer of my heart: *Goodbye.*

Epilogue

ARE YOU WONDERING IF Gertie was a real little girl? And if her real life adventures really happened? You don't have to wonder any longer. Yes, Gertie was a real little girl; and, yes, her real life adventures really happened.

As the dedication page explains, it was the childhood memories of the author's mother—the Gertie of this book—that inspired *Gertie's Real Life Adventures*. True, the story is fictionalized and the names of the characters changed, including Gertie's and those of her family. But the events, like her riding the elephant in the circus parade, working in her folks' restaurant, her baptism in the horse trough, Indians asking for "brawa" at the kitchen door, befriending a mentally handicapped child, hauling buckets of water from the spillway, and "volunteering" for the Novocain demonstration are all true experiences of her life in Richfield, Utah, in the late 1800s early 1900s. While these events are fictionalized, the *spirit* of Gertie is not.

But what about Gertie after the end of her Real Life Adventures story? Did she have other adventures? You be the judge.

When times became difficult and the Richfield Restaurant failed to provide the means for caring for the family's needs, Gertie and her family left Richfield and traveled to a gold prospecting site in the state of Oregon, not to pan for gold, but to make their living doing laundry for the prospectors. Mama Larson boiled the prospectors' clothes in a huge pot over an open wood fire, with the family helping. Some years later when Gertie was in her teens, the family moved to California. There Gertie, her mother, and her sister, Pauline, toured the vaudeville circuit as a musical trio. Gertie played lead mandolin, Pauline played second mandolin, and their mother the guitar. In the accompanying photograph, taken to publicize their act, Gertie is seated on the left, her sister on the right, and their mother standing behind them.

Epilogue

As Gertie grew older, she married and raised a daughter, a rather subdued adventure compared to her earlier ones. Then came World War II. While Gertie couldn't serve in the military, she could volunteer to help in the war effort. And volunteer she did. Part of the week, she operated a switchboard at the Red Cross center, freeing Red Cross personnel for more critical duties. Many Friday and Saturday evenings she worked at the Salvation Army and U.S.O. canteens, in the kitchen, making and serving sandwiches and coffee to members of the military. And, yes, washing dishes.

Then when she was in her sixties, her husband passed away. Her daughter had married. Gertie was on her own. So she went to work in a factory making rubber parts for the space agency. Some of the parts she trimmed and sanded ultimately landed on the moon. On her 70th birthday, the mayor came to the factory to honor her for her years of employment. Her picture appeared on the front page of the local newspaper.

Finally, at age 78, she retired with the best attendance record of all the other employees.

Twenty years later, at age 98, she left this world for the most exciting adventure of her life. She passed away peacefully in her bed at her daughter and son-in-law's home, looking forward to meeting her Lord and to seeing the glories of heaven.